# A SPARROW

# IN

# THE

# SNOW

# A SPARROW
# IN
# THE
# SNOW

SYLVA DAREL

Translated from the Russian by
BARBARA NORMAN

SOUVENIR PRESS

First published in the U.S.A. by
Stein & Day, New York

First British Edition published 1974 by
Souvenir Press Ltd, 95 Mortimer Street, London W1N 8 HP

ISBN 0 285 62106 8

Printed in Great Britain by
Clarke, Doble & Brendon Ltd., Plymouth

*To My Parents*

*A SEGMENT OF A LIFE*
*IN FOUR ACTS*
*WITH A PROLOGUE AND*
*AN EPILOGUE*

*Prologue*

# CHILDHOOD

According to my mother, I was born in a luxurious establishment, "run by Doctor So-and-So himself," she used to say proudly. Again according to my mother, the first words she said after my arrival were:

"Which is it?"

"A girl."

"Nothing missing? Hands, legs, head?"

"All there."

"Whoof! Give me a cigarette."

It seems I forced my way into this world out of sheer stubbornness; that's the kind of character I had. There was no getting rid of me, I came right in, unwanted.

"There was nothing I didn't try!" Mother said. "A bath so hot I passed out. Jumping, first from a chair, then from a chair on a table. Then I drank all sorts of horrors, jumped some more, risked breaking arms and legs, and boiled myself in the tub. But you hung on like a leech, there was nothing doing. What I went through when I realized nothing was going to work! I was afraid I was going to bring a monster into the world, but it turned out all right. You were an adorable baby, though a handful even then. Always hungry, always bawling. Nurse used to call me at the store and hold you up, wailing, to the mouthpiece to summon me to my maternal duties. I'd run over to nurse you, and two hours later it would start all over again as if you were more bored than hungry. You could never be left alone for a second, unlike your sister. Now she was a quiet one, plump and contented. She'd lie for hours under the table lamp jiggling the glass beads on the shade. They'd tinkle, and there she'd lie, smiling happily. But you couldn't be put off with glass beads. With you, it was rock me, sing to me, carry me!"

"Why?"

"I don't know, that's just your character. You were mischievous—very amusing, it's true—but I didn't have time to entertain you. Maybe that's why you were so mean. When I nursed you, you chewed me up so badly, you had to be put on bottle feeding. You started talking early, your teeth grew in early, and you learned to walk early. Oh, the things I've gone through with you!"

That's what I heard all my life. I was always trouble. There was a time when I seriously believed my contrariness was the result of all those attempts to keep me out of this best of all worlds.

Mother was rocking me on her lap, singing something in German in her smoke-husky voice. I was nine then, but I still liked this kind of sentimental foolishness at times. It was then I first discovered you could force your way into God's world if you were stubborn enough . . . That was in Siberia. There were four of us living in the hut.

"My God, to think you could have not been born at all. Lord, how could I have lived without you?"

"But how could I not have been born when I was already alive?"

"There was nothing I didn't do to stop you!"

Naturally I didn't understand how boiling-hot baths or jumping off a table might have spared the world my existence, but I believed Mother. With a spasm of love and a pang of conscience, she promised to get a spoonful of cocoa from someone the next day and cook it in practically pure milk. Lord, how nice it was the baths didn't work . . .

My parents were well off. Father had the biggest dry-goods store in town, an interest in factories of some sort, and the two-story summer cottage on the Riga coast. He had something somewhere else, too.

My sister was older than me by one year, nine months, and eighteen days, and this caused me no little grief until I realized success does not depend on seniority alone.

We had a good, kind nurse, but she didn't know any foreign languages, and what intelligent, bourgeois child can get along without French or English? So governesses appeared, all known as "Mademoiselle."

Each summer we went to the cottage, just five minutes from the sea through the woods. We loved it. And it's there my memories begin.

Mademoiselle insisted we behave properly and made us walk hand in hand, but there were a thousand distractions in the woods—bilberries, mushrooms, heather, birds, an occasional porcupine, squirrels leaping, and the sea waiting beyond. Hand in hand indeed! We'd run wild and get a lecture on how little girls should be proper and obedient.

None of our governesses liked the sea; they all found it cold. As for my sister and me, it was hard to drag us out of the water. I can still see a thin figure in hat and stockings hailing us from shore with futile reminders about Papa and Mama having arrived from town long ago, supper getting cold, disobedience being a sin, and spoiled children disgusting. When we finally crawled out, we'd be blue and covered with goosepimples. They'd dry us off with towels, dress us rather carelessly (I always managed to get my head and arms stuck in my dress), clutch our little hands tightly, and bundle us home with giant steps.

Every now and then, we weren't allowed to go to the sea. Our governess would choose a sunny clearing in the woods, lay down a newspaper, then an old blanket, and undress, spreading out every bit of clothing carefully. She used to smooth out her blue or cream-colored slips lovingly and conceal them between the newspaper and the blanket. Her corset she bashfully kept hidden from us.

Then came my first crime and punishment. The governess doted on her slips, and I didn't like her telling me what to do, so I shoved a handful of bilberries under the blanket. How she cried when she saw the huge purple spots. I felt very sorry and ashamed. I got spanked at home, but the governess left anyway.

We had a lot of governesses, but except for that episode, I don't remember much about them. All of them used to run along the shore, rant about cold water and nasty children, and complain to Mama in the evenings.

Once my cousin came from abroad for a short visit. He drove us by car along the beautiful road by the sea to Libau* to visit Grandmother and Grandfather. Bouncing beside him on the front seat, I was utterly happy. He wore a white shirt, and I was all dressed up, too. Then the car broke down. Everyone was tired, my cousin's shirt was no longer white, the sleeves and front covered with grease. I wanted to go to the bathroom, but was too shy to say so, everyone was so cross. It grew dark. I hid and was soon discovered with wet panties. I wished I was dead. A passing car took Mama

---

* Now known as Liepāja.

and me to Grandmother's, where they washed me, standing naked in a big tub and whimpering with shame and sorrow.

At age four, I went to kindergarten—a French one, of course, run by Madame Chateau. My sister was then starting first grade in a French lycée. Our kindly old nurse came back to us, so we spoke Latvian with her, German with our parents, and French to each other. From time to time, we were taken to the movies to see Mickey Mouse or Shirley Temple, but I liked the zoo and the circus best. At the zoo, a monkey once snatched my white straw hat off my head, along with a little hunk of hair. I was about to bawl with fear, then was overcome with delight. At the circus, I always hoped the wild animals would jump out at the audience instead of doing what they were told.

We used to get into mischief at the summer cottage. We had great fun, though our pranks sometimes ended badly. Behind our cottage were some trees and a big green meadow, where we used to do gymnastics with our teacher. We had a swing there, a hammock, some little benches, and a sandbox. There were sheds, too, for garden tools, wood, and coal. One day I found a wasps' nest in the corner of one of the sheds and brought my sister and two neighbor girls to see it. They watched openmouthed while I poked a stick in the center of the funny paper cylinders, so skillfully stacked on top of one another. We sprang, yelping, out of the shed, but the wasps burst right into the house with us, buzzing angrily in our hair and biting through our clothing.

I was stung hardest by the wasps, which obviously knew I was the one wielding the stick; also, I had been closest to the nest. I rolled on the rug and screamed, whimpered with resentment when they spanked me, and started yelling again when I looked in the mirror and saw my nose, lips, eyelids, and even my tongue all swollen.

There was a wonderful orchard behind the house with huge cherries, almost black and very sweet, and lots of berry bushes and vegetables. The scent of ripe tomatoes, smelling of sun and freshness, especially when you snap off the stem, has always brought that garden back to me.

The gardener was a good-natured old man. He used to arrive in the morning, water the grass and flowers, clip bushes, cut flowers, sprinkle fresh sand on the walks, and harvest the crops. Probably his most difficult duty was making sure the owner's children—we, that is—didn't eat unripe, unwashed fruit and vegetables. The poor man couldn't tie us up or stand watch over the garden all day. One day I put my sister up to "helping" the gardener. We knocked down more than two pails of cherries with sticks, but they weren't ripe enough for jam. All were wasted.

That wasn't the worst. The plums were considered ripe when they were covered with a bluish film like a cloud. There wasn't any film yet, but I was sure the plums were ripe. For two hours, my sister and I stuffed our tummies with them before we doubled up. We were soon ready to howl with pain, but restrained ourselves, having correctly concluded that since the plums were probably to blame, we would do better to suffer in silence. However, it wasn't long before we started bellowing. Mama came rushing back from town with the doctor. Dysentery, he said. I don't remember the pain at all, but I remember very well Mama not going to work in the morning for a long time, the doctor coming twice a day, and their holding my jaws open to pour in castor oil. My sister got well in three weeks. I had the bad kind, the doctor said. Mama sometimes cried while sitting beside me, and

I'd take advantage of her mood to beg her not to give me castor oil and grated apple.

I didn't die, but I got so thin I had nothing to sit on except little bones. While I was convalescing, they often put me on a couch out on the terrace. Right above me in a corner of the roof, was a swallows' nest with four naked little birds chirping in it. What fun it was to watch them. The mama and papa swallows would take turns flying with a chirp into the corner, and all the baby birds would at once stretch out their skinny, naked necks with open beaks. Like clockwork, the parent would put the food right in the beak of the young one whose turn had come. Though I was still blue-tinged, the little birds were putting on weight and growing up before my eyes. Often they would fall out of the nest and hop frantically over my couch. I'd squeal with excitement and send for the grounds keeper and his stepladder to put them back. The birds soiled things, too. They'd swing about in the nest, lift their little tails, chirp, and a tiny dab would drop right down on my leg. The whole performance was completely absorbing.

By then, my sister had been well a long time. Mama later told me I'd been on the brink of death. If that's true, it was certainly the most comfortable brink I've tottered on, because my only unpleasant memory is the castor oil.

In 1939 we came back from the seaside earlier than usual so I could start school in the French lycée on Henri Barbusse Street where my sister went. I was delighted. We had always failed to celebrate my birthday, the tenth of September, because of the trip. Either we were just getting ready to leave the cottage or we had just arrived in the city.

I remember our last evening at the cottage. The fireplace was lit in the big living room, and the folding doors between it and the dining room were open. Papa, Mama, and some other people were sitting tensely, with serious faces, next to the radio in the dining room. The station played the English national anthem, then the French. Sister and I knew them and started to sing along, but the grown-ups hissed at us. Papa raised his eyebrows significantly and pursed his lips. It was war. The grown-ups talked in low voices, and we became quiet, too. From that day on, Papa was preoccupied—calculating, reckoning, making up his mind. But he calculated too long; it was soon too late.

I had no free time anymore. I went to school—by now, I could read and write (in French, of course), sing songs (also in French), and I took ballet and music besides. I was said to have talent and facility in ballet. As for music, my technique could be developed, but I had little gift. Never mind, an educated bourgeois child had to be "able to play Chopin, at least."

My technique never got good enough for Chopin, but I used to play chopsticks rapturously with my bony fingers, and when the piano was confiscated, my latest, and insurmountable, musical challenge was Beethoven's "Für Elise." I didn't get much farther in ballet, though I danced twice in an adult ballet on the Opera stage, where we children did a better job of getting underfoot than showing off our skills.

We lived in a large, six-room apartment on Shkolny Street across from the Italian embassy. Below us lived the owner of the building, an enthusiastic hunter. He had a dog, a setter bitch named Taiga, white with brown spots. I knew she had had puppies, and, overcoming my shyness, I rang his bell one day. I was shown into a kitchen, which smelled like the zoo. Under the big kitchen table lay the beauty, Taiga, with four absolutely unbelievable puppies swarming and wriggling around her. I rushed toward them and was ecstatic when Taiga licked me in passing as if I were one of the pups. My parents were surprised to hear how hard it had been to tear me away from the puppies. But I got worse. At every appropriate and inappropriate moment, I pestered my parents for a puppy. Poor things, they thought I could be put off with promises. Even when the puppy had been forced out of them, they had no idea what was in store.

"Buy me a puppy and I'll be a good girl," I promised, and believed it.

"I'll practice the piano hard if you give me a puppy," I promised, knowing it was a lie.

"I'll eat everything on my plate if you just buy me a puppy," I promised, with reservations.

"I'll go to bed every evening without making any trouble if you'll buy me a puppy," I swore.

I don't think my lavish promises really made much of an impression on my parents, though my most convincing argument was the one about eating, a matter that habitually led to painful scenes and sometimes blows. I couldn't even look at eggs, the sight of butter sickened me, and I hated soup, not to mention kasha. I was punished by spanking. The procedure was always the same. Anna, the cook, who loved me dearly, would grab me, scratching and wriggling, put me over her knee, pull up my skirt, pull down my panties, and flourish birch twigs dipped in water, touching my behind with them now and then. Each time they touched me, I would groan from the pit of my stomach, roll my eyes, and try to bite Anna. None of this had solved anything, but perhaps a puppy . . .

That was my first taste of truly great happiness. He was waiting for us when we came home from school—a tiny, golden-brown, silky spaniel with long ears down to the floor and such an adorable muzzle that I don't know who licked whom the most.

My poor parents! Eating, sleeping, and studying were out of the question. I thought I'd go out of my mind with happiness. I was even jealous when Sherry, as we named him, licked my sister more. I shook as if feverish and was afraid to leave Sherry for a second. My parents were at their wits' end. They kept trying to put us to bed, but as soon as our door closed, Sherry would begin whimpering in the hallway and waddle up to the door. Either my sister or I would sneak into the hall in our long nightgowns and carry Sherry back to bed. There were puddles in the hall, the beds were wet, too, but Sherry would become quiet at once under the covers and we would lick each other happily. My parents would overhear, discover Sherry, and turn him out. We were awake all night, whispering, "Sherry, Sherry," and listening for our beloved's pitiful whimper.

In the morning, my parents looked solemn and angry. They got my sister off to school with some difficulty; with me, they failed. I rolled my eyes, wheezed, coughed, pretended my throat hurt, and, oh joy! I was found to have a temperature. What a happy day I spent with Sherry. I rocked him in my arms and sang him a Latvian lullaby, "Aya Juju Lachou Bearnie." I ate, too, just to show Sherry how good children eat, when he refused to lap milk out of a saucer. That evening my parents looked solemn and angry again. And that night was a repetition of the first, with us whispering, him crying, puddles everywhere, and the beds wet. In the morning, they didn't bother taking my temperature, they packed me off to school "without any argument."

I could hardly wait for classes to end, but when I got home, Sherry wasn't there. He had disappeared. The apartment was quiet and empty. That was my first taste of great sorrow. They had taken away everything that would remind me of Sherry, his basket, bedding, and saucer, but the smell was still there, such a warm smell that I wept softly and bitterly, and felt again, with my whole trembling body, Sherry's silky, warm, wet nose.

Back to the seashore for the last time, for "soon things were going to be very bad," we gathered from the grown-ups' worried conversations. All they talked about was the "Reds" and how they had come into the city on tanks with red flags and called it "stretching out the hand of aid and friendship." Father's face grew pinched. He often came home from the city during the day, and sometimes he never left the house at all. He'd lie with a wet cloth on his forehead, suffering from a migraine headache. He drank soda for heartburn.

Mama used to come back from town in the evenings looking worried. Father would rush to meet her, she would explain something to him in detail, and he would express dissatisfaction. They always waved us away. That summer, we were left to ourselves for the first time; we even went down to the sea alone. In the evenings, we were packed off to bed early. Because almost none of our former neighbors had rented that summer, we had nowhere to go. We went back to the city earlier than usual, too, but even so, my birthday wasn't celebrated. I didn't insist because the grown-ups' concern had spread to us, too.

We learned they had confiscated Father's store, that at first they wanted to have him work there, but then turned him out completely; that Mama was working as a clerk in the clothing department; that they had ordered Father to pay a huge tax, but he had refused. My parents spoke Russian together so we wouldn't understand. Often they whispered. As a matter of fact, they whispered most of the time in the house of late, even with friends, even on the telephone.

We felt the change in the lycée, too. We no longer sang Latvian, French, and English national anthems in the auditorium in the mornings. Classes began right off, without ceremony. There was less French, more Latvian, and Russian was introduced in the upper grades.

It was spring, 1941. One day when we got home from school, we found Mama crying in the courtyard and a truck parked at the back door. Some fellows were dragging a piano through the narrow door. Our piano. And the truck was full of our furniture. Tears were rolling down Mama's cheeks. She patted my sister and me on the head. We stood very quietly, understanding nothing. This was called the confiscation of property.

Next they "reduced our living space." They moved in a Red commissar, a woman who was a distant relative of ours. We liked her at once; there was something so mysterious about the words "commissar" and "Communist." She had an admirer who was also a Communist. I could never get used to the idea that the big living room was no longer ours and often forgot to knock. Once, rushing in without knocking, I saw our Red commissar sprawled on the ottoman, her arms spread out, her eyes closed, a tangle of legs, and her admirer lying on top of her and biting her lips. Terrified, I rushed out of the room with a wild shriek: "Mamochka, Papochka help, Uncle's eating up Aunty!" That was my introduction to sex.

I had a happy childhood on the whole. Little sorrows are quickly forgotten. Sometimes, years later, I would think back on some childhood incident, not as a simple fact, but as a clue to things that weren't as they should be. For example, I learned very early that my parents didn't get along—"If it weren't for the children, they would have separated."

"My parents insisted on my getting married, I would never have married him for anything," Mama used to complain. Still a tiny thing, I'd climb on her lap, whimper out of solidarity, and dry the tears rolling down her cheeks. Of course we didn't know the reasons for our parents' disagreement, and many, many years went by before I stopped blindly taking Mother's side.

Another vague memory was of Father coming back from abroad. Mama, my sister, and I, all dressed up, went to meet him at the airport. We were standing on the field; my mouth was open with excitement, and I shrieked when the plane flew in, rolling across the ground, and Papa suddenly came out of it. I exhausted the grown-ups with questions about how the plane could travel in the sky and what it rode on when you couldn't even see the ground from up there. A mystical feeling about planes has stayed with me even though I studied basic aeronautics later on.

Later, in Siberia, I'd think back on the joys of holidays at home, the holiday table, or decorating the tree, as if they were the illusions of delirium. I remembered Father and some other men sitting in hats at the table, saying something in some completely incomprehensible tongue, giving us something sweet that smelled of honey, matzoh, and other strange foods, and sending us to bed early. We also shared the joys of Christmas with our non-Jewish friends. There was the dance program we put on, smearing our cheeks with cranberry jelly, dancing a sailor's dance and a doll dance. There was the buying and arranging of toys under the tree, the distribution of presents, the squeals of delight—I often dreamed of this many, many years later.

Mama's dressing table also made a profound impression on us. When my parents went out in the evening, my sister and I used to play "two ladies." We'd put on her silk stockings, stomp about in her high-heeled shoes, and literally disappear in her perfumed dresses. And with serious faces and great skill, we'd ravage the little jars, vials, and tubes. We always got a scolding afterward from

Mama, who discovered the pillage by the runs in her stockings and the powder scattered all over her bedroom.

Another thing we loved was riding the tiger and the white bear. The tiger was in the living room, and the bear in my parents' bedroom. We used to sit on their heads and gallop off, but the tiger and the bear were confiscated with our other belongings.

Soon came that night of the thirteenth of June, 1941, when we heard a long, loud, terrifying ringing of the bell. And thus, before I was eight, my happy childhood came to an end.

# SIBERIA

We stare at each other wildly; my sister's eyes are wide. The bell is still insisting, loud and terrifying. We hear footsteps running. Then strange voices. And Father's voice, convincing, confident.

We sat up in bed. Mama came in, very pale, and told us to dress. We didn't ask her anything. For some reason, she was opening and closing the cupboard, getting out our schoolbags. Some strange men came into our nursery, searched for something, even leafed through some books. One softly told Mama in Latvian she'd better take warmer things and warm blankets, with winter coats for the children. Mama threw up her hands, moaned, "Where are we going for that long?" but no one answered. She packed one suitcase carefully, then another. She got out our handsome wine-colored winter overcoats, tied blankets and pillows in a big bundle.

Papa kept talking, no longer very convincingly; now he seemed to be asking, gesticulating, searching the strangers' faces, even smiling. He kept asking to be allowed to call someone, to make certain of something, but they told him the telephone was cut off. Then he, too, hurried to get things together. He packed his shirts very carefully, took a few suits off the hangers, walked around the room with them, and hung them back in the closet. He began sweeping up ties, putting lots and lots in a suitcase. Mama grumbled but packed the silverware on top of the ties, six of everything. Papa took several pairs of suspenders and some initialed handkerchiefs, while we stuffed our schoolbags with French books.

Then they led us downstairs (it seems they allowed two hours for gathering belongings). There was a truck below with frightened people sitting on bundles and suitcases. We were loaded on, too, and the truck drove off. All over the city we came across cars and trucks, the trucks all headed in the same direction. We stopped at the railroad tracks, where several freight trains were standing. They unloaded the things, took the people off, and began herding them into the trains. The cars were nothing like the ones we used to ride in to our summer cottage, and the train was terribly long and had no engine. The cars were red outside, with a sliding door and a bolt in the middle; there were no steps, and you had to reach up high. In the center of the car was a hole in the floor.

Papa found us a place on the planks that lined the car in two rows. Go to sleep, he told us. How was anyone to sleep? It was all very interesting and not a bit frightening. There were children younger than my sister and me in the car, so tiny even, that their mothers held them wrapped in swaddling clothes. I'd never seen such little ones before. Papa had stationed himself at one of the four little openings and was keeping watch. From time to time he'd suddenly shout to someone in Russian, and get an answer back. He kept asking and arguing, but was apparently unsuccessful, threw up his hands, and gave up. However, he still kept watching for something.

The second day, a friend of Mama's brought us a small bundle of bed linen and some food. Mama, speaking very loudly, tried to get something across to her and shook Papa off angrily when he interrupted her. We were still standing in the same spot the third day, when the door suddenly opened and they called Mama. She came back very upset, saying she'd proved her proletarian origin and shown she was a worker, not a bourgeoise or some other dangerous person, and they'd therefore made an exception and given her permission to stay on with the children. But she had refused because she was afraid for us to stay without Papa; in exile, at least, we'd all be together.

On the fourth night, our train pulled out. For three days and three nights they had been loading the train with people carrying bundles and suitcases. For the first time, I knew what hunger was. My sister and I were starving, but food was brought only once, by Mama's friend. People kept running alongside the trains, calling out names, looking for one another, and crying.

Traveling was very interesting. There were lots of people in the car, each busy with his own affairs. From time to time the train stopped, the bolt rattled, the door slid open, and women would run up selling all kinds of goodies. Father would bargain, buy, and we'd gobble it up. Everything tasted unbelievably good. They had given us a pail and we collected a few glasses among us. Father ran after boiling water whenever we stopped and generally took charge of the car.

There was no toilet, and the hole in the floor could be used only when the train was in motion. The guards bawled us out if we used it at stations, where we would stop for hours at a time. I was embarrassed, but Mother screened me with a sheet.

Latvia came to an end. We were crossing Russia. No one came up to the car with roast chicken or meat pies anymore. Everything looked poorer, more ramshackle, there were no bright flowers in the gardens, and the picket fences were not so brightly painted. Then people escorted by soldiers began bringing up cases of canned fish to sell. The writing on them was in Russian. Besides Papa and Mama, no one in the whole car understood Russian, but only Russian was spoken around us now. So Father bought food, made complaints, and asked favors for everyone.

Suddenly we started passing military units. The soldiers sat in open freight cars, swinging their legs, singing to the concertina, waving to people standing on the platforms. We were often stalled for hours because of them. Then we learned war had begun a few days before; Hitler had attacked on the morning of the twenty-second of June.

Hunger was the only thing that bothered us children, the rest was wonderful. Sometimes the train would stop in the middle of fields, the bolts would rattle, and children, twitching with impatience, would jump out, shrieking with joy, and rush to pick flowers or swim, if there was the tiniest pond deep enough in sight.

There were no steps on the car, and once, when I jumped out, I fell down a high embankment. My arms, legs, and face were scratched and my knee pretty deeply cut. You could even see something white through the blood. I began yelling, not from pain, but because it looked so frightening. Mama came running, terrified. Father was worried, too, and asked for a doctor, but the soldiers laughed, and one recommended soot instead of iodine. Papa ran to the engineer, and we smeared the knee with soot. I whimpered every chance I got so I wouldn't be scolded for jumping out. The knee healed quickly, leaving a black scar you can still see.

We studied Russian on the journey. The first word was "pilchards," a kind of cheap fish, which I pronounced *beechkee* instead of *bweechkee* because I couldn't say the Russian letter ЬІ. There was no such letter in any language I knew. They used to bring us cans of things like fish in tomato. Then came milk, *moloko,* which I mispronounced because of the absence of the hard *l* in languages I knew. Sometimes the soldiers would talk to us. Afterward, we'd question our parents, but they didn't understand much of the soldiers' vocabulary.

And then, on our second frightening night, the bolts started rattling and we woke up in terror. Cries, shouts rang out. The train was standing still. An officer appeared in the opening and shouted:

"All men out!"

My father rushed over to him.

"Why men only?"

"No talking. I said, all men out!"

"But there aren't any men, just women and little children and some old men. I alone take care of them all, there are lots of sick, some dying."

The officer obviously didn't believe it, but was too lazy to climb up and check. He shined his lantern around, and, in fact, all he saw was the heads of children, and women frozen with fear.

"Lock up, the devil with them."

Ours was the only car in the whole length of the train with some men left. Father looked proud and took charge cheerfully. It seems they were still gathering men up from some trains, putting them in others, and sending them to various concentration camps in the Komi Republic, Pechora district, Solikamsk, and even Kazakhstan. Few survived. Many years later, in Siberia, the wives and children learned how quickly their menfolk had died of hunger and cold. The women pursed their lips tightly and made remarks about men's weakness and women's endurance.

In the car people whispered about the war, what bad luck it was to have missed staying free by just a few weeks, how much trouble they'd seen and what still lay ahead, and how they might have just gone on living in Riga, now long in the hands of the Germans, with whom they would somehow have come to terms.

The weather was splendid that summer, I don't remember a drop of rain. We had already been traveling over two months. It was mid-August.

Then, once again, at night, we heard:

"Out of the cars with your things—march!"

The bolts rattled, the door slid open.

"All out, with your things!"

Father rushed over to the soldiers.

"What's this? Where are we to go at night, in the dark? We have little children here, sick people, people are sleeping."

"Shut up. I said, all out!"

"But where are we? What are you planning to do?"

For the third time, I woke up with my heart pounding so I thought it would burst with fear. Mama was trembling, children were crying. The grown-ups thought they were going to shoot us.

We were unloaded into the night. Not a light anywhere. We climbed down the embankment and sat there on our bundles and suitcases. It was cold. My teeth were chattering and I was whimpering quietly from fear. Father wrapped me in a blanket and took me on his lap. How funny it looked in the morning, with all those people sitting, lying, walking about; lots of people, and not a house in sight. Except for the embankment and the railroad tracks, there was nothing around at all, just a bare field, and, everywhere, people, people, people.

This was camp. No food, no water, no light, no shelter, but the grass was green, the flowers and butterflies so beautiful, and the sun shone on everything, warm and good. No one made you practice the piano, no one did anything, we could loaf around wherever we pleased. It was great!

The day went by, the night went by, the grown-ups were in despair.

"How long are we going to sit here under the open sky? We've got to do something."

"What if it rains? I don't even have an umbrella."

"It's not really so cold in this dreadful Siberia."

"Just wait, it's only August."

Father, pursing his lips, was thinking something over. No one paid any attention to us children. We discovered a lake and swam in it until we turned blue.

On the second day, however, carts approached us. Then came our assignment to kolkhozes, or collective farms. The kolkhozniks left their horses at a distance and walked through our camp, looking, discussing, appraising the goods and families. The moment they saw old people and little children, they'd walk away.

Our turn didn't come for a long time. We slept on the ground another night, but there was boiling water and food now. Papa had built a sort of hut for shelter at night. We met people we knew. Mama even found her best friend, who'd been traveling in another train. Her husband had been taken away. In fact, there wasn't a single man left in their group, and it was lucky her son was only fourteen. They brought their things over to join us.

Our turn came at last. Father fussed, rained questions about the kolkhoz, and negotiated, while Mother tugged at his sleeve to tell him to agree quickly and not drive up the price as if he weren't glad to be taken with two useless mouths to feed.

The road ran through fields and woods, past a lake; the sun shone, birds sang, queer pine cones were scattered around, grasshoppers chirped, dragonflies fluttered. We romped like puppies. "Don't lag behind," we were warned.

It got dark quickly in the woods. I became frightened and asked Father to carry me. Though he must have been terribly tired from walking in his city shoes, he still wouldn't sit in the cart. He did not want to appear weak before the kolkhozniks, who walked behind the cart all day, only climbing up to eat while the cart moved on. The women glanced at me with pity, as they unpacked their bundles. Perhaps I looked dolefully at them, I don't remember, but they gave me the biggest chunks of flat bread. Perhaps I was the smallest.

The next day we reached the kolkhoz of Alexandro-Yersha, Dzerzhinsky district, in the region of Krasnoyarsk. A very kind woman took in our family, along with Mother's friend and her son. She heated up a pot of pea soup with cracklings right away, and gave us some delicious village bread. We couldn't understand either the children or the grown-ups. People laughed when my sister and I tried to say something to the village children in a mixture of three languages plus hands, feet, and face.

Father disappeared briefly. When he came back, he declared he had found "a splendid place—a real paradise," and without further ado we went on the next morning to another kolkhoz.

The "paradise on earth" we reached toward evening turned out to be kolkhoz Mokry-Elnik. We moved in with "Aunt" Nastya Barlovskaya, with whom Father had made an agreement earlier. We slept on the floor, all in a row. When we woke up in the morning, the hut was full of people. They were sitting in the doorway and by the stove, standing, leaning on the wall right next to us—women, young girls, even a few men, all staring in complete silence. Mother fidgeted under the

covers, obviously wanting to get up, but embarrassed
to appear in her nightgown. Papa managed a smile,
though a sheepish one, while my sister and I jumped
out in front of everyone in our long nightgowns down
to our toes. Oh what that set off! They began talking,
clucking like geese, pointing at us, clutching at us, and
fingering our nightgowns. They kept asking us something, but we only wriggled in the women's arms. Mama
asked the men to turn away. They understood and tact-
fully left. At the sight of Mama's nightgown, our audience
was thunderstruck.

"Good Lord, a dress like that she could take off at
night . . ."

"To think, somewhere people live like that . . ."

"Why'd they come to our miserable mudhole?"

"They're rich, you can see that, but they haven't
brought much with them"

"And the children are thin, sleeping in silk or not."

"Look, look, she wears a wedding ring."

"Oi, dearie me, him too, him too."

"They really live."

"And her hands are so white, not roughed up, and
what fine fingers!"

"You couldn't earn a day's pay with hands like that.
What are they going to live off?"

"And as if you can live off the fat with a day's pay
anyway . . ."

"But I've got a cow and more than wormwood growing in my vegetable garden . . ."

"Oh, the poor creatures, the troubles they've got, and
with little children, too. They don't even talk like us,
do they?"

The women bent over our bedding, fingered the blankets Mama had put on the floor in place of a mattress,
crumpled the sheets in their fingers, and smacked their
lips in admiration, talking among themselves.

Papa pulled on his trousers under the covers and crawled out briskly to get acquainted.

Alexandro-Yersha was gigantic compared to Mokry-Elnik, which had only about 50 huts. One, at the edge of the village, barely bigger than the others, was the school.

Several days before school started, Mama took us to the school, where she met the very pretty teacher and registered us, but she made a mistake. When asked how many years of school I'd had, she said one. So they registered me in second grade, though I'd only gone to pre-school, but they didn't know what that was. Therefore, when I came to school on the first of September, all the children were older than me, and already knew how to read, write, and sing songs, while I hardly understood any Russian. I still used to cry at that age. Mama taught us the alphabet at home, talked to us only in Russian, and in a couple of months, you couldn't tell us from the village children. We got top grades, *fives*. Then Mama decided we shouldn't neglect our French. How she groaned when she found out we'd forgotten everything already. We couldn't read or write, and all that sticks in our minds to this day are some songs and verses: *J'ai du bon tabac dans ma tabatière* . . . and then something about a nose and tobacco . . . and that was all.

When we'd been living with Aunt Nastya a month, the kolkhoz assigned us a hut in the courtyard of the stables where they kept the foals—one room with a big wood-burning stove and a lean-to. That was a very happy time for me. The stable man used to come in the mornings to feed and water the foals, and when I appeared half asleep in the doorway, all the foals were galloping across the courtyard, tossing their tails. I used to gallop right after them. The youngest ones loved me, the older ones sometimes bit or tried to kick, and mostly for good reason—I kept trying to ride them.

The kolkhoz gave us firewood so that when the cold came, the hut was very cozy. My parents worked in the fields, but they didn't get food for it. The kolkhozniks kept count of the workdays for which they were supposed to give us something at the end of the year ("if it isn't all taken away," they always added anxiously).

They went out to the fields early every morning, Papa in trousers with suspenders, a shirt with a tie but without a jacket; Mama in a silk dress and high heels. Papa worked the threshing machine on the threshing floor. Mama cut wheat with a sickle, tied it in sheaves, piled them in stacks, then loaded them on carts. She cut her legs with the sickle, her sheaves came undone, even an ordinary rake gave her blisters; her stockings tore, her dresses got snagged, and it was very awkward working in high-heeled shoes. She found it a little easier when one of the kolkhozniks brought us bast sandals. Mine were especially pretty because I tied them with hair ribbons instead of with string.

We bartered things for flour, potatoes, and milk. Soon the young kolkhoz girls were dancing to the concertina outside our hut in Mama's long pink nightgowns, wearing their high boots, with kerchiefs tied right over their foreheads. Mama was awfully embarrassed.

"I told them those weren't dresses, but they didn't believe it. Now I have to suffer for it, watching them."

"But Mamochka, it's so pretty, and they dance and sing so nicely."

"There's nothing for you to fret about," Father consoled her. "If Grizodubova herself could walk out of a store in a nightgown and not be embarrassed going around Riga in it, it's quite all right for a kolkhoz. Too bad you don't have any more nightgowns, they gave us more flour for them than for anything else."

"And who was Grizodubova?" I asked.

"A pilot."

"A woman pilot?"

"Yes, but not just any pilot, a famous one. I don't know exactly, but I think there were three of them and they set a world record. When the Reds took Riga, all sorts of celebrities began arriving from the Soviet Union."

"And then what?"

"Nothing. Why do you ask?"

"What about the nightgown? Why did she walk around town in a nightgown?"

My parents exchanged glances. I knew that meant "It's none of your business."

"And what business is it of yours? She liked it and walked out in it."

"They're to sleep in."

"Well, she didn't know it was a nightgown, she thought it was a dress."

"How could she be so famous and not be able to tell a nightgown from a dress?"

"What did you know about bast shoes before? And not long ago, what did I know about using oven tongs and pincers? I'd never laid eyes on them. That's the way it was with Grizodubova," Mother argued.

"We didn't need tongs and pincers at home, we had a gas stove. You only need tongs for a Russian stove, but everybody sleeps in nightgowns. How come she didn't know?"

I kept insisting because I could see my questions disturbed my parents.

"Stop it, you unbearable child. Because the Soviets grabbed everything, because they didn't have any such beautiful things, because they'd never seen the like. Do you understand?"

"Yes. But why?"

"What do you mean, why?"

"Why didn't they have all those things?"

"I don't know," Mama said crossly. "I told you to leave me in peace."

"Mamochka, don't be angry, just answer one question for me and I'll stop. Which is easier to cook on, a Russian stove or a gas stove?"

"A gas stove."

"Then why don't they have gas stoves here?"

"Because there isn't any gas."

All in all, we were in luck in that kolkhoz. The people were very kind and treated us well. From the very first, the women used to come in the evenings to sit a while, bringing a loaf of bread or a jug of milk or sometimes a pail of new potatoes. They gave us a small kerosene lamp, too, explaining how to use it. The women gave Mama lots of advice.

"Don't be afraid of the stove, just don't poke your head inside, learn to regulate it with a broom or a poker. And use the tongs, don't pick up the iron pots with your hands, they take a long time to cool off, that's good, old-fashioned cast iron."

Someone gave us a kneading trough, too, and the women showed Mama how to mix dough and knead it. "It's not enough for your head to sweat, your bread is ready when your backside is wet." But Mama was exhausted before her backside got wet, and the tenderhearted women finished kneading the dough, cleaned the hearth stove with a wet broom, brought cabbage leaves to lay under the loaves, and showed her all the ways to tell the bread was done.

The women made fun of Mama for a long time after she looked down a well in horror and said, "How would I ever get out of there?" She thought you fetched water by going down in the well.'

My sister and I were covered with swellings. At first we thought they came from mosquito bites because the midges and mosquitoes ate us up mercilessly. Mama even scolded us, thinking the bites swelled like that because we scratched them. But when she saw huge, festering boils, she got frightened. The boils hurt, itched, and generally interfered with enjoying life. They took a long time to go down and left an ugly scar if you picked at them. I still have a dent under my knee from one of these carbuncles.

Then we learned about lice. Mother didn't know what lice were, but she told someone in the village that the children kept scratching, especially at night, and that she had found some strange bugs in the sleeves of our night-gowns. Could they be the ones that were biting?

As Mother told us later, the woman looked at her with pity as she said, "Those are lice, my dear, lice. Not part of the good life. Tell me, do the children's heads itch, too? You have to learn to hunt them out—to take a knife, hunt, and kill. And crush the eggs too, keep after them, because they hatch into lice."

"But where am I going to get a special knife like that?"

"Use an ordinary one, all the villagers hunt lice like that. You won't get them all, but there will be less scratching."

We only had one knife, one that was given us. Mother was keeping the silver ones to sell. It didn't matter, she got used to working on our heads with the table knife. She had to.

News of the war reached the kolkhoz at the end of September with the first death notices. Almost every family had someone at the front, and all the villagers were related to each other besides. It seemed as if the whole village was in mourning at once. Everyone used to wait for the postman with great impatience and fear, and over and over, the women would come running from the fields, stumbling, wailing, and wringing their hands on hearing the terrible news.

We learned what we could about the situation at the

front from the meager information in the local newspaper, a single small sheet called the *Dzerzhinsky Worker*. The kolkhoz had no radio. Sometimes a month-old issue of *Pravda* reached the kolkhoz administration. Nearly all the adults left in the village were illiterate. They used to gather around the kerosene lamp in the administration building to hear Father read the newspaper aloud.

The kolkhoz chairman, a disabled man named Sitnikov, used to visit us from time to time with his wife. The war situation was discussed too, along with doubts and anxieties. Even questions were sometimes ventured. I remember Sitnikov asking Father what the world was coming to when completely innocent people with little children could be taken away from their homes and driven to some miserable hole where there was neither house nor home. I remember how horrified they looked when Father told them how many exiles there were on the road.

That October, the first snow fell, fluffy and pure, the kind that doesn't melt, and it made the village look very pretty. Our hut was warm and cozy. Mama was beginning to get the knack of firing the stove. The bread rose, more often than not as a good housewife's should. We acquired felt boots, shawls, a mat on the floor, and a twig broom to keep at the entrance for brushing snow off boots.

Completing the cozy picture was our pet Yuki, a frisky, fluffy, gray kitten I'd fallen head over heels in love with at Alexandro-Yersha, our first kolkhoz. When Papa found our present "paradise on earth," Mokry-Elnik, I stammered that I had to bring my kitten, but they just scolded me. We had left early in the morning. By noon, my coat pocket and my entire side were damp. I had to take the kitten out of my pocket to dry off. My parents even stopped the horse to discuss the situation, Papa rolled his eyes furiously and Mama squealed, but neither of them could remain serious. I looked too funny with my crestfallen face and the crumpled ball of fur with its thin, wet tail. Yuki and I won.

Once again they came at night; banging loudly on the door, kicking it with their boots. We heard men's voices. Father struck matches over and over, too drugged with sleep to find the lamp wick. I heard my heart pounding with terror. Three strange men burst in with the chairman of the kolkhoz.

"Name, patronymic, surname, date of birth."

Father answered, then began talking quickly, quietly, explaining, gesticulating.

"No talking. You're under arrest. Start the search."

Two of them ripped open our straw mattresses and pillows, rummaged through our suitcases, even emptied out our school briefcases.

Papa couldn't keep still.

"It's a mistake, dear comrade, a mistake, it can't be right—a man works in a kolkhoz, earns his living by honest labor, gets his grain, firewood, and potatoes, while his wife works herself to the bone in the kolkhoz fields, and there are little children—he can't leave, they'd be lost alone."

"Shut up! Put your personal property on the table, it's subject to confiscation."

The hut was freezing cold at night. Mama put our overcoats on us and stood sobbing, hugging us to her. We began sniffling, too. The kolkhoz chairman stood rigidly by the door, eyes fixed on the ground.

Papa got dressed, put together a change of underwear, a toothbrush, and a piece of bread, and kept tying and untying his bundle as if everything depended on it. His hands shook. He looked at us, his eyes wet, lips trembling, chin jerking. When it came my turn to kiss him good-bye, I suddenly hung on his neck and cried,

"Papochka darling, why are you leaving us, don't go, how are we going to live without you?" Mama and my sister burst out crying loudly and Father, too, but the men tore me away and pushed Father out the door.

We sat beside Mother that whole horrible night, the second of January, 1942, sad, frightened to death, unable to understand.

HOW I LOST MY FAITH IN GOD*

I'm sitting on the stove bench. The stove takes up half the hut. The hut is just one room, without even a lean-to. We, the owner, and a calf live in the hut. There are three of us, Mama, my sister, and I. The owner is called Grandmother Kima. The calf lives with us because he was just born and Grandmother Kima's cattle shed has no doors. The cow spends the night with someone else in the village.

The calf is a funny sight, tethered in Papa's ties. When he was born and they brought him home, he lay down, then got up on his thin little legs, swayed, and began wandering all over the hut. Granny Kima couldn't find any string to tie him in the corner, so Mama knotted a few of Papa's ties together, wrapped them around the calf's neck, and tied him to a nail. He's still lying there, wrapped up in ties. It's very funny.

As for me, I'm sitting on the stove bench. In front of me is a big, yellow, wooden box, a round one, with a lid. Mama said she used to carry hats in the box. Now there's a whole treasure in it, six breads. It's true they didn't rise—"Is this supposed to be flour?" said Mama—but that doesn't matter, they're just as good.

Mama's been gone for two days to find out where

* This story was written when the author was thirteen.

Papa is and what's happening to him. My sister's playing outside, but I just wanted to sit. No one can see me, the stove bench is screened off by an old curtain of Grandmother Kima's. I'm sitting there, quiet as can be, thinking. "Six breads. There were fourteen. Yesterday we ate six, this morning, two. Soon Sister will come in, and we'll eat one more each, and when Mama comes back in the evening we'll give her two and eat one each ourselves. Mama will be very pleased we didn't eat everything up like locusts and not leave her anything . . ."

I'm a punishment, not a child. Earlier this winter, we lived in the kolkhoz hut, not with Granny Kima. They gave it to us because we had Papa, and he was a man, a worker. But when those men took Papa away, the kolkhoz took away our hut. Grandmother Kima let us move in with her for money. When the foals bit and kicked me when we lived in the kolkhoz hut, or when I skinned my nose or my knees, Mama always used to sigh and say I was a punishment, not a child. She often says that.

That's what I'm thinking, sitting on the stove bench. It's very quiet, there's only the calf suddenly taking such a noisy breath it sounds like a sigh. And then I think about God. I know God can do everything, and I'm thinking that if I were God, I'd make the six breads into, maybe, ten—and cook some potatoes, too, even just boiled in their skins, and I'd get so generous I'd add a bit of herring and sour cream. I often think back on a lot of good things, but I didn't want to eat them then. They even used to spank me to make me eat, and I'd cry and drive Mama to tears. Now Mama says if I'd eaten like a human being then instead of forever making trouble, I wouldn't always be so hungry now. She always brings in some animal as an example, a camel or maybe a snake, because it seems they digest their food over a very long time and aren't forever asking for something to eat.

I know God is very busy. He has lots of poor people on his hands and there's a war on, he's helping defeat the Fascists, and God has lots of other business besides that I don't know about because I'm still a little girl. When I grow up, I'll know everything. But I love God now just the same and never reproach him, even when I'm very hungry or skin my knees badly.

The door squeaked, I hope it's my sister. She's older than me and unless she tells me I can, I'm not allowed to touch my own bread. But it's not Sister, it's Granny Kima. I peeped around the curtain because she was being so quiet, but she was there. She crossed herself in front of the icon. She crosses herself every morning and evening and also whenever she leaves the hut for a long time, and she whispers something while crossing herself. Once I stood next to her and started to cross myself, too, but she pushed me away and said I shouldn't mess around with her God. I said everyone's God is the same. But Mama interrupted and explained that though there's only one God, there are different religions. I didn't mess around with Granny Kima's icons again, but I didn't understand this about different religions.

Suddenly a hand reached behind the curtain. Granny Kima groped for our round box, drew it to the edge of the stove, opened it, fumbled inside, and took out a bread; sighed, took out another, closed the box, and pushed it back into place.

I froze, overcome with horror, and shame, too. I was so ashamed for Granny Kima that it didn't occur to me right away that Mama wouldn't get her share now. I was so afraid Granny Kima might see me on the bench. How ashamed she would be then, it was horrible.

But Grandmother Kima didn't see me. It was quiet. I peeped out. She was crossing herself in front of the icon again, one hand clutching our bread. And then I felt as if something had hit me right in the stomach. What about God? Didn't He feel sorry for Mama, and

me, and my sister? We have no hut, no cow, no calf,
even no Papa. That's why He's God, to know all this.
Could He see it and not do anything? It would be so
easy. Grandmother Kima could have seen me right away
when I first peeped out, and then everything would have
been avoided. Or the box could have been where she
couldn't reach it, God had plenty of resources, that's
why He's God. He could have saved our bread. That's
the way I believed in Him.

Grandmother Kima left. Suddenly, for no special
reason, I burst out crying. No one had beaten me, no
one had scolded me, no one was after me, yet I cried,
at first quietly, then louder and louder, feeling so outraged that by the time my sister came in, I was bawling
at the top of my lungs, howling, even.

That evening again I felt outraged and started crying
loudly because my sister told Mama I had eaten the bread
and Mama looked at me very reproachfully. Once again,
God did nothing, though He could have.

I stopped believing in God, though I didn't say anything to Mama about it. Sometimes I turned to Him out
of habit in difficult moments, but it was only out of habit.

In summer, our kolkhoz came to life. The grown-ups
worked in the fields and vegetable gardens, the children
ran around like crazy, and there was no end of things
to do. We organized raids on the peas, turnips, and car-
rots, hunted mushrooms and berries, and sometimes
helped the grown-ups.

Spring was the worst time. The cattle were hungry,
the hay ran out, and there was no grass yet; the firewood
was gone, there had been no vegetables for a long time,
and hardly anyone's flour had lasted. We ate repulsive,
slimy cabbage and soups of oats and water. The kolkhoz
chairman and brigade leader yelled at people in the morn-

ings, knocking loudly at the windows to get them off to work. There were not enough seeds, not enough working hands, and one after another authorities came from the regional headquarters, threatening, poking their noses into everything; they, too, had to be fed.

But summer—that was great. The cows gave more milk and there were berries and mushrooms. Once I fainted from sheer pleasure. Our neighbors, the Sokolovs, had a few beehives. The grandfather, one-armed Grampa Lesha, built a kind of honey factory in the vegetable garden. He would put the honeycombs in a barrel, and when he twisted a handle, liquid honey from all eight combs flowed down the sides of the barrel to be tapped by a faucet at the bottom. Once they filled a whole bowl with honey for me, let me pick fresh cucumbers right out of the garden, and told me to dip them in the honey. Cucumbers often turn out bitter, but they can't be wasted, and with honey it doesn't matter. The aroma of cucumbers and honey made my head spin, and it seems I fell down right there in the middle of the vegetable bed. When I came to in the Sokolovs' hut, the first thing I said was, "Where's my honey?"

The women used to take me to the woods to hunt bilberries. You could pick a lot in a day, but I wasn't strong enough to carry a full pail and I had nothing to take along to eat for a whole day. The women used to give me snacks. Mama would exchange the bilberries I picked for milk or potatoes since we had nothing to keep the berries in for winter. Soaked, frozen bilberries are very good in winter; you use them with boiling water in place of tea. If you had sugar you could make jam out of them, too, but there was neither sugar nor tea in the village. The women used to talk about a time, before the war, when there was a store in the village that sold matches, thread, kerosene, salt, and other household necessities. Sometimes they even had cotton cloth for dresses and polka-dot kerchiefs. You could take butter and eggs to town and buy sausages and meat with the money you got. Suckling pigs and poultry and calves were sold in the town market, too, they said, and there were always potatoes, and meat was not uncommon, even in the village.

I listened to all this talk skeptically. How could all that have existed once, when the children at school used to make fun of my sister and me for speaking of buttered buns and cocoa and bananas and grapes? They simply refused to believe us, and, little by little, we forgot such things had existed. How could memories of such tasty things last when salt was scarce and soap was a problem? Mama was always complaining that we kept growing and had nothing to put on, and her own silk dress was in shreds. Maybe there once was cotton cloth in the store and polka-dot kerchiefs; now there was nothing. The women wove sacking themselves, made skirts out of it, then made jackets out of old skirts, and patchwork quilts out of old jackets.

Some villagers kept two or three sheep. The sheep didn't give milk and there was nothing to feed them in winter and spring, but the women and girls used to spin yarn out of the wool. I loved watching them spin. They would gather in someone's hut on winter evenings, each carefully drawing a thread from her bundle, and sing nicely in harmony. I began to imagine I could sing, too. Children usually weren't allowed in the hut where the young girls met to spin, and if they did let us in, it was no farther than the doorway, on the floor. As soon as I started howling, they'd chase us out. Everyone used to be on guard for the moment when a vocal inspiration would overtake me.

Even though Papa had been taken away and Mama wasn't the best worker, the women treated her well. They often came to her for advice or just to sit and talk. She was considered well-informed, particularly on medical matters, and, in fact, she sometimes gave helpful advice. In return, the women would bring us half a dozen eggs or some milk or a loaf of bread. I even remember one old woman bringing Mother a sick hen for advice. In view of her ignorance of chickens' diseases, Mama solemnly advised the woman to chop off the hen's head. Mama also filled out official forms and wrote letters to the front for the entire village. The old women felt especially sorry for my sister and me. They used to look at me—puny, skinny, with legs and arms like a spider—shake their heads, and sigh.

"And why should these little ones suffer? What kind of danger are they supposed to be? To whom?"

They couldn't understand Mother's explanation that we were "socially dangerous elements." Frankly, neither did I at the time.

There were all kinds of inconveniences. For example, there were no toilets. Some people had little outhouses, shaped like birdhouses, in their vegetable gardens, but Granny Kima didn't have even that. There was no fence around the house either, just a cattle shed without doors. When we had to go to the bathroom, we'd make sure no one was coming down the street, jump into the shed, and be as quick as we could so no one would see. Mama always minded it, but we didn't at all. Naturally the shed was never cleaned out, and you never went far from the entrance, or you'd get stuck in the mud, especially in summer. And winter wasn't much better. The mud froze in slippery lumps and we often had to dig through the snow to reach the shed. Huge snowdrifts used to pile up overnight, even inside the shed itself. The villagers got around the problem more simply. I often saw some old aunty, walking down the single village street, stop in the middle of the street and do her business without squatting, barely adjusting her skirt. Then she'd walk on, leaving a sharp hole with yellow edges in the icy road.

Washing was another problem, since bathhouses weren't common, either, by a long shot. Usually a few neighbors would heat a single bathhouse in someone's vegetable garden and take turns. All the baths were heated "black"—that's when there is only a kind of half stove, made of bricks, with no flue or stovepipe. A cauldron was placed on the stove, and under the cauldron firewood was burned, and the smoke went right in the room. Water was brought from the well, and there was a wooden barrel in which cold water was kept to mix with the hot. Often there wasn't even a separate room to undress in.

The villagers felt sorry for us and took turns letting us use their bathhouses. Mother tried very hard to bathe us at least once every two weeks, but she didn't always succeed. I could never get used to the smoke. Sometimes Mama would start to wash me and I'd faint. She'd dry me off as fast as she could, and drag me out in the fresh air. The villagers used to let us bathe when they themselves were through so it was no longer very hot, but we just weren't used to that kind of bath. They used to raise still more steam by splashing cold water on the hot bricks, and they'd whip each other with twigs. Often in winter, the women and children, naked, red, lashed with birch twigs and well steamed, would jump out of the bathhouse right into a snowbank, roll in the snow, and run back in again. But no matter how hard Mama tried, my sister and I still had lice. Whole armies foraged about in our hair.

School we loved, and the teacher, too. She was the sole instructor for four grades, studying in two shifts: first and third, then second and fourth. As a result, my sister and I not only got on each other's nerves at home, we sat in the same room in school, too. Second grade was in one-half of the room, fourth in the other. The teacher used to walk among us explaining, asking questions, checking homework. By the time I reached fourth grade, I was already familiar with many of the things taught in it.

There were only a few textbooks for the whole class, but we traded them back and forth and sometimes did our lessons all together right after class. We didn't have real notebooks. Every sheet of white paper was used for letters to the front, so we wrote between the lines of old newspapers that we would sew into rough notebooks. If only we'd had ink—but that was lacking, too. We used to mix ordinary stove soot with water. It would run on the newspaper, and our teacher often had to ask us what we'd written because she couldn't make it out. It is odd that though we learned penmanship under such crude conditions, both Sister and I have fairly decent handwriting.

One day Mama took a trip to Dzerzhinka, where our regional kolkhoz office was located, in order to inquire about Father. I think she was trying to find out if he was alive or not. In the administration office, they told her exiles were being sent still farther north, to the Igarka area in the Polar Circle. Mama was very upset, but exiles she knew in Dzerzhinka told her about a woman in the administration who could help if she wanted to. Mama still had a few knickknacks left, so she gave the woman a pair of stockings and a very pretty embroidered silk case in which she used to keep her nightgown. We were constantly threatened with being sent north, as so many people actually were, and Mama had to bribe that woman more than once.

The summer of that year, our second in Siberia, there was a big event in our kolkhoz. For the first time ever, a truck suddenly appeared in the village. All the children ran openmouthed after it, my sister and I, too. The driver stopped the truck several times to ask something; the children hung on the running boards, yelling and giving directions. There was a second man sitting in the front seat. The truck stopped at our Grandmother Kima's house and the second man climbed down. The driver handed him two suitcases and drove off.

We stared at that man as if he were a miracle. And he stared back at us. Suddenly he walked right up to my sister and asked her name. He looked somewhat strangely at me, too. We were both frightened, but, on learning who we were, the man burst into tears. Mama was running from the fields by then, and she started crying, too, as she hugged him. He was Papa's brother from Moscow.

Only much later did I realize what kind of man he had to be and what it meant to undertake a trip like that in that terrible wartime to search Siberia for the unknown wife and children of his brother, "an enemy of the people." He had had no contact at all with our father for many, many years. It was dangerous to have a brother abroad, particularly when you worked in a ministry in Moscow, even in the paper industry. Uncle spent one whole day with us. He and Mama could only talk late at night because the entire village came to look at the miracle from Moscow, and there was no chasing the children away. We were bursting with pride that even *we* didn't have only bad things happen to us.

Uncle brought us enough wealth to take care of almost a year's living. He left us writing paper, pencils, pens, wrapping paper, money, and food. It was a great event. Mama sold the paper sheet by sheet, and for the first time, we had something other than old newspapers to write on in school. And real ink.

My sister had to continue studying, and there were

only four grades in the village. Mama took another trip to Dzerzhinsk to see the same woman in the administration office, and she managed to arrange for us to be allowed to move there. The kolkhoz let us have a horse, the women helped us load our mattresses and other household goods on the cart, and they even saw us off. What concerned me most, of course, was Yuki, who didn't want to stay in a dark bag, but the villagers said we shouldn't let her see the way or she'd run back. Everyone in the village escorted us to the outskirts, even the lame kolkhoz chairman. The women hugged and blessed Mother and kissed us. Everybody cried.


DZERZHINSK

The first thing Mama did was take us to school. We were late for the start of classes, but they accepted us. My sister was registered in fifth grade, and I in third. There was every reason to be glad, but I clung to Mama. Though my own foolishness made me miserable, I begged her not to leave me alone because the children were all so big and self-assured and well dressed, and couldn't I, perhaps, be sent back to the village? And if not, it wasn't at all necessary that I go to school, too, a learned sister would be quite enough. I could see Mama felt sorry for me. She seemed somewhat lost herself in that big, two-story school with a principal, a director of studies, male teachers, and even a special staff room. All this after our one-room village school with one woman teaching all four grades! When I had almost persuaded Mama and could already see us going home together, a young girl, barely taller than me and wearing a very pretty, bright-colored coat, suddenly came up to us.

"Are you new?"

"Yes, but I don't know yet if I'm going to study here."

"What grade are you in?"

"Third."

"Oh, how nice! You're in ours, then," and taking me by the hand, she dragged me down the hallway without giving me time to say good-bye to Mama.

She settled things in the classroom by simply shoving a little boy out of one of the desks, tossing his books, notebook, and other things into his arms, and sitting me down beside her. She was Lyusya, the prettiest, richest, and smartest girl in class. Her mama managed the only bakery in Dzerzhinsk, her papa was a commissar at the front, and they had been evacuated from Moscow. I felt shy with her, but very proud of our friendship, though I had nothing to boast about—Papa, Mama, or where I was born, because Mama had told me very sternly before we left home not to say anything.

"Lyusya, why do you wear your coat in class?" I said to make conversation.

"I have the prettiest coat in the whole school. That's for one. Second is so it won't be stolen. They steal everything—pens, pencils, and the bread and butter out of our bags. If you do as I say, I'll give you a bite of my sandwich, or even a whole sandwich. We have lots of bread."

I was too shy to thank Lyusya, but I felt reassured.

Dzerzhinsk was much bigger than Mokry-Elnik, where we had stayed before. Besides the secondary school, there were an elementary school, a real club where they sometimes showed movies, a hospital, and even a square where a market was held on Sundays. There was also an orphanage right next to our school.

"But don't you dare have anything to do with them," Lyusya told me the very first day. "All the orphanage children are thieves, they're always hungry and very bad. When they fight, they bite and scratch. They're like wild animals because they don't have any parents."

I stopped being afraid of school and fell in love with Dzerzhinsk. Everything was more interesting there. Mama was better off, too, because she knew lots of people among the exiles. She also had more problems, though. Things had been simpler in the village. Here, she had to pay a lot for a room, and food was more expensive. We were growing out of everything and had nothing new and no possibility of buying it. Mama had a very hard time. But she never reproached us for anything, just asked us to study more, ask fewer questions, never argue with anyone, and, in general, God help us, refrain from standing out in any way.

Mama had changed a lot in one year. Two days before our arrest in June, 1941, she had turned thirty-six. She was very beautiful, elegant, gay, and witty then. She had come from a poor family and hadn't had an easy life when young. She married at her parents' insistence, not for love, but money brought no special happiness either. Papa detested what he called "squandering." Everything he did was planned in advance, every penny was counted. Mama's whims were very sparingly indulged, but she managed by stealing a bit from her cash register.

In Papa's store, he was lord and master, feared by all, while Mama was cashier and good fairy. Mama had all kinds of fur coats and lots of diamonds, but Papa wouldn't let her wear them: "Never draw attention to yourself." Papa demanded moderation in everything. The fur coats hung in closets, smelling of mothballs; the jewels were laid away in various hiding places. Papasha didn't spoil his children either. He taught us to save at an early age, giving us two pennies every day with a speech on how hard it was to earn money and how it should be saved. We saved it up and bought Mama presents on her birthday.

Mama had been in Vienna, Berlin, Paris, I think, and once went to Karlsbad for a cure. I remember how pleasant it was when we visited her with Papa in the most elegant sanitorium on the Riga coast, in Kemeri. Now she was all alone, without money, without a specialty, unused to physical labor, and with two children to support. She scurried from morning to night looking for food, for work, and trying to "look decent." We were little help, particularly me. I hadn't been an adorable child for a long time, and my sister caused no little trouble, too. Also, we were forever hungry, and who were we to ask for food besides Mama? She sold her own and other people's things, but the last to go was Father's watch that he'd somehow managed to pass to her when he was arrested, though it was subject to confiscation, too. There was no paper in Dzerzhinsk and there were illiterates. Mama sold paper by the sheet and wrote letters and applications for people. We moved four times because Mama was always looking for a cheaper room. Each was smaller and worse than the preceding one. The last was a long, dark mud hut where there were four of us because we shared it with a young woman in order to live cheaper.

The townspeople were different from the villagers. Accustomed to exiles and evacuees, they took advantage of the newcomers' poverty. For that reason, I remember the kind exceptions particularly clearly.

Through people she knew, Mama managed to get a job as charwoman at the grammar school my sister and I attended. The heavy classroom desks had to be carried out for the daily washing of the floors, the water was ice cold, there were lots of classrooms, and the hallways were endless. Taxed beyond her strength, Mama became thin and weak. The floors weren't washed to perfection, remarks were made to her, and she leaned over backward trying, out of fear of losing her job.

Mama had a worker's card, we had our dependents' cards—together, we got eight hundred grams (just under two pounds)—of bread a day. Then the ration was cut to six hundred and fifty grams, but even this much was not easy to get. We took turns standing in line for bread at night, first Mama, then my sister and I. We often missed school because of it, and sometimes we'd stand four hours in the fierce cold and then the bread would give out. Sometimes, the moment the salesgirl announced the shortage people would stampede into the shop from the street, thrusting puny children like me out of line. The bread was bitter as can be, made with wormwood and bran.

My most unpleasant memories of hunger are connected with Dzerzhinsk. Mama used to make "cabbage soup" out of grass. She cooked potato peelings, made a watery porridge with bran, and a kind of pudding out of the waste from cattle silage. This last delicacy was almost as hard to get as bread. We'd go at night with pails to the gates of the building where they made the leavings of oil pressings into cakes of fodder for cattle, and we'd find ourselves at the tail of an enormous line. In the morning, they'd start distributing a pail per person of the cloudy, sour, brownish, liquid waste. We used to cook it with starch, which was also a scarce item, and pour it into basins and bowls, one per head. My head often refused to accept this pudding, hungry though I was; or, rather, my head would accept, but my stomach refused. Sometimes I exchanged my bowl with my sister for a fourth of her portion of bread, fifty grams, which made both of us feel we'd gotten the best of the bargain. I, at least, wouldn't get sick that day, and my sister had two whole bowls of that repulsive swill. I didn't quite reach the end of my rope then, but I got so thin my skin was blue.

At the Sunday market in Dzerzhinsk, they sold frozen cabbage, fresh and in sauerkraut, frozen milk slabs, sunflower seeds, cedar nuts, and resin sticks for a ruble each.

The resin helped make hunger bearable. You chew it until it crumbles into dust, the resin smell fills your mouth, your jaws work, you click it for fun—and you don't feel so hungry. Mama used to exchange even our old underwear for food at the market. She sold old things for other people, too, and they'd give her something for it. She kept her job only to be eligible for a bread card and so we'd get our dependents' cards, because if the head of the family didn't work, dependents weren't given cards either. Uncle's money didn't last long. Usually there wasn't enough to pay the rent. For a while, we lived in one room with the landlady and her two sons, one of whom went to school. The landlady sometimes asked us to feed the younger one during the day while she was at work. I systematically ate everything she left for the poor child, out of principle: Set a wolf to keep the sheep . . .

Mama often complained she couldn't sleep for the bedbugs biting her at night. I remember spots on the pillows, sheets, and walls, but I don't think I suffered particularly from bedbug bites. The lice bit us mercilessly throughout our stay in Siberia and neither "head-hunts," nor boiling our clothing, nor any other measure brought relief. We'd get fewer swellings but there were always one or two that wouldn't let us live in peace.

The children from the orphanage went to our school, where they made up more than half the class. The poor things were even worse off than we were because they had no one to stand up for them. They moved about like shadows, eyes on the floor, looking for crumbs and seeds in the cracks, all dressed in gray overalls, faded and patched. I visited them in the orphanage. The long, cold corridors were lined with trestle beds with blankets of the same gray. There, too, the children shuffled around, barely moving their feet, and if they spotted something on the floor, they put it right in their mouths.

They all had shaven heads and hungry but indifferent expressions. The orphanage staff used to steal their bread and exchange it for other things so the poor things were deprived of even their meager shares.

Lyusya and I became friends. She was very clever, and I listened to her. Her family had a big home with beautiful things, and were only five in three rooms: Lyusya's mama, who managed the bakery, Lyusya and her younger brother, her grandmother and grandfather. Lyusya used to eat the bread and butter she brought to school underneath her desk cover because the orphans begged so for it. To tell the truth, I often stared hard at her mouth, too, but she used to give me a piece and sometimes brought some extra buttered bread along especially for me. She was a year older than I, prettier, plumper, and cleverer, and therefore took me under her wing. Lyusya knew everything.

Two other girls, Valya and Ira, became friends with us, too. Valya's mother was also a manager of something. My mother sold Valya's mother our shorts right after we arrived. Later, when we danced the "Moonlight" or "Troika" in evening amateur performances, Valya changed from pink shorts to blue ones for the "Troika" while I had to dance without a costume.

We began having boyfriends in fourth grade. It started by my getting a crumpled note on which was scribbled: "I love you. And you?—Little Bull." I was horrified. Little Bull was the smallest but meanest boy in class. He was always fighting, pulling the girls' braids, and often ran around butting his head in people's stomachs; he called it "taking them head-on." His head was big and round, though he was very small, that's why he was nicknamed "Little Bull."

I decided to consult Lyusya. She understood everything, and had already told me something about love.

At recess, we four friends got together, each holding an identical note with a different signature: Little Bull, Shaitan, Molchan, and Khrush. All were nicknames or diminutives.

"Do as you like, girls, but I love my Khrush," said Lyusya. "Khrush is the best-looking boy in class."

It was true. Volodya Khrushchev was not only the handsomest, he was the oldest. In six years, he had only gotten to fourth grade. Terrible stories were told about him. For a bit of lard, two girls from the orphanage, twins named Shura and Olya, were supposed to have done something awful with him on the clubhouse porch.

"My Molchan is just as good," Valya pouted. "And his Papa is an NKVD official. When he grows up, he'll be an official, too. And my mama says they live very well. I love him."

"I'm scared of Shaitan," said Ira. "He really is like a shaitan, his legs are crooked, his eyes burn, and he has such a lumpy head. And he fights so. I think I don't love him."

My turn came.

"What does 'I love you' mean?"

"Haven't you ever been to the movies?"

"Yes, so what?"

"Every movie has something about love."

"I've only seen two movies and there was no love of any kind, but there was a very good story about a dog on a border post. They called her Dzhulbars, and she caught enemies and all kinds of spies."

"Stop talking nonsense, we're fed up with your eternal dog stories."

"I saw another picture, too, also about spies, called *Thirteen*. That was in the kolkhoz. They showed the film right on the street and it broke down all the time and when it started to rain we didn't stay for the end, we all ran home. So I don't know if that one had anything

about love. It was just about us and the counterrevolu-
tionaries."

"It's about love when they kiss at the end of the film,"
Lyusya said.

"Who kisses?"

"Why, he and she."

"Do you absolutely have to kiss if it's love?"

"Of course, otherwise how would it be love?"

"And when am I supposed to kiss Little Bull? At the
end of what?"

"He'll let you know."

"But I don't know how to kiss. Only Mama kisses
me."

"I'll teach you," Lyusya promised.

In a businesslike way, we began discussing how to
answer our admirers. The note to Lyusya made it clear
the answers were to be put in strict secrecy in a cupboard
near the coatroom at the end of the corridor before school
was out. Lyusya wrote a form answer, "I love you, too,"
and told me to write the same thing. At first, I resisted.

"I don't want to kiss him, which means I don't love
him. Besides, I'm afraid of him, he's always hitting me
on the head."

But Lyusya explained, "When they love you, they
always hit you. That's how they let you know. And if
you don't answer the note right, he'll hit you just the
same, but harder. So write it quick."

I wrote. Lyusya talked about love with great
enthusiasm and I listened with great interest.

"This is just the beginning. The next note will say,
'Let's become friends.' I've already known all this a whole
year. I became friends with Slava Tarasevich. He was
very handsome, but they were exiled north last summer."

Little Bull had a thick stick. He hopped around the
desks with it, hitting the girls. After the note, the stick
struck my head particularly hard—Little Bull was express-

ing his love. I hated him. We "became friends." In the mornings when it was still dark, and more often than not on the river ice I had to cross to get to school, Little Bull would suddenly fire a barrage of snowballs at me from behind a snowdrift. He would make them in advance, squeezing them hard so they'd hurt. In school, he beat me with his stick, pulled my braids, and spattered my face and clothes with ink. When I walked home, he'd suddenly swoop down on me out of nowhere, hit me on the head with his schoolbag, and knock me down, or butt me into a snowbank with his head. I'd run away, howling with pain and anger.

This love affair went on until summer. The following year, Shaitan, who until then had been in love with Ira, fell in love with me. My Little Bull and Lyusya's Khrush were repeating fourth grade. The boys hit us less now, but new motifs appeared. The notes were, as always, the same to all four of us. The latest had a mysterious message: "We love you, give us." I'd gotten some ideas about love even though Little Bull and I had never kissed either at the end or in the middle, but now they were asking us to give something. Lyusya lectured me angrily for being so dumb and made a sketchy drawing of what they were asking us for. I didn't understand.

"What for?"

"What do you mean, what for? I don't know exactly, but people who are in love have to do this."

"And where will we give it to them?"

"They'll let us know."

"I'm not going. They can hit me all they like, I'm not going. I'm scared."

"You fool, there's nothing to be scared of."

"How do you know?"

"None of your business."

"I'm not going. I'm afraid of Shaitan. He has yellow eyes, crooked legs, and thick lips. I got in trouble with

Mama when I was still a child and we played 'one-two-three, pants down' with little boys and looked at each other. I'll get in trouble now, too. I know this is something bad."

Ira suddenly took my side. "I'm not going either. My mama also told me girls should never play with little boys, never let themselves be touched or looked at. Mama won't let me undress all the way in front of my brothers. And I've heard that's how children get born."

"You're a fool, too," Lyusya said indignantly. "You can't have children until you're thirteen and we're only twelve."

I didn't answer the note. Shaitan hit me hard, pricked me with a pen, and poured ink over me. I was afraid to complain. I had trouble on all sides, from Shaitan, the teacher, and at home, from Mama, because of my stained dress. I used to cry often then.

Unlucky in love, lucky in something else—unexpected good fortune struck us. Through some organization or other, Mama's sister in Palestine found out where we were and started sending packages from time to time. Mama sold absolutely everything in the packages, even the blouses Aunty sometimes sent especially for us. Mama's customers were managers like Lyusya's and Valya's mothers, salesgirls in the bakery, and a few other women. Sometimes Mama sold things to a woman doctor she and the other exiles worshipped. She had an odd name, Iran or Tigran (she was Armenian). We gave her the nickname Ranty-Granty Granovna. Because Mama praised her so highly, she took a special interest in us, and we idolized her, too. I used to look rapturously into her weary, dark, slightly bulging eyes, and I was very fond of her dark little moustache and the white streak in her dark, curly hair. She lived in a little house on a hillside near the hospital, a good piece beyond our school, almost in the woods. Mama gave Ranty-Granty goods for which we got milk in exchange, and I would go to collect it every other day. Sometimes she'd let me in the house to get warm. Sometimes she even gave me a bowl of delicious soup that tasted like meat broth. Kindly Ranty-Granty used to stroke me on the head and feel my ribs, shaking her head. Then, no doubt because my ribs stuck out more than they should in her medical judgment, she'd pour me a whole jug of milk though we were only entitled to one liter. I'd drink down my "rib" bonus quickly, right there at the door, without the slightest twinge of conscience.

Winters were so cold the trees around Ranty-Granty's house made loud cracks like gunshot. On days like that, especially toward evening, I sometimes found the bodies of frozen sparrows lying on the ice of the River Dzerzhinka or right on the snow. They told us in school that birds often freeze while flying because the cold penetrates their feathers right down to the body in flight and the heart freezes. I was sure the sparrows would live if I could just get them warm. I'd bring them home next to my chest, breathe on them, wrap them in rags, and be furious when Mama threw them out in the snow in the morning. But Mama explained that if a sparrow took flight in such cold, it was because he had to, had to so badly he would die just the same if he didn't fly. So he was better off flying with hope than shrinking in fear.

I was afraid of crossing the river on the narrow path beaten down in the snow. It was dark. The wind blew fearfully and strongly. The fingers I had frozen in Mokry-Elnik got very numb with cold, I couldn't feel my feet under me from cold and fear, and I had to clutch the jar of milk to me so the milk wouldn't freeze. Once it slipped out of my hands and broke as it landed on the ice. I was so horrified, I fainted.

It seemed to me I was asleep, warm, and comfortable. Then someone shook me, and my face burned and hurt a little. I thought I heard a voice. It was so pleasant, I didn't want to open my eyes, but I did because they started shaking me hard. I was lying on a bed with people standing around me and a strange woman rubbing my hands and feet with snow. The snow raked my skin, my body felt as if boiling water were being poured over it. An entire family had brought me back to life, it seems. They found me on the ice, thought I was dead, but brought me home all the same to try to revive me. I laughed with them when they described how they'd shaken me, while I, lazybones, continued to pretend faint just to frighten them. Later we all had very sweet hot tea. When I took my leave I told them that Mama would give me a bad scolding for breaking the jug and spilling the milk. They gave me a full jug of milk, and accompanied me home.

That same winter, Sister came down with measles. I had had it long ago in Riga when I was little. Because children come through measles better than adults, they had put my sister in the bed where I lay, covered with a repulsive red rash, but she didn't catch it then. And now, at thirteen, she'd suddenly come down with it in cold and hunger, when there was no doctor and no medicine of any kind. As we had very little firewood, we wrapped her in all our clothes and blankets. Still she groaned, shivered, and screamed at night, and Mama kept feeling her forehead and running around the room in despair. We gave her a little cranberry juice mixed with water to drink. I tried to amuse her by making funny faces, but she just groaned and wouldn't open her eyes. I thought then she was going to die and told Mama so. Mama ran to the neighbors for a sled. We wrapped Sister in all our blankets, put pillows around her, and dragged her like a sack of potatoes up the hill to the hospital. The sled was terribly hard to pull, especially uphill. Mama cried, but the tears froze her eyelashes. To keep from crying, she started shouting at me. I wasn't much help dragging the sled, she said; I would do better to help push the sled from behind, and keep close watch to see if Sister was still breathing.

We left Sister in the hospital with Ranty-Granty, who cured her in a few days. When we came back for her with the sled, we skipped happily and quickly down the hill.

Another time, Sister caught her foot on her felt boots and chafed it (or rather, she chafed it on her leg wrappings; apparently she hadn't wound them on right). Her heel started to swell. It hurt and bothered her, but she didn't complain much and still got around somehow. Then suddenly, a broad red strip spread along her leg below the knee, stopping at the knee bend. It became painful and swollen, then her whole leg swelled so she couldn't bend her knee, and under the knee was a dark, festering canker. Mama said that couldn't go on, that she'd send my sister to the hospital in the morning. But that night Sister began screaming and writhing. Her body was covered with sweat, she was burning all over, and she shouted that her leg throbbed right up to her head. Once again, we dragged her over the ice on the neighbors' sled to our Ranty-Granty. This time, Sister had to have an operation. Mama and I waited, frightened to death, in the hospital corridor. Ranty-Granty came out looking very angry and told Mama it was a disgrace to have let it go like that, they had almost had to cut off the leg. She expected everything would come out all right, though they'd had to cut and clean it out. Because there was still some inflammation, she said, it would be a good idea to get hold of a certain new medicine. Mama left me alone to go after this medicine with a special authorization from one of the NKVD, or secret police, officials, but she was unable to get it. And Sister got well without it.

I had my painful moments, too. For instance, Valya had bought our shorts but wouldn't let me dance in them. And the little boys teased me. One, younger than I, was especially mean to me. He was always sitting on the fence when I came home from school. In winter, he threw snowballs; in summer, pebbles, always shouting, "Latvian, Latvian!"

"Shut up, you fool."

"Latvian, Latvian, exile, deportee."

"And you're a Yid, sitting on a mud fence."

That startled him into silence. Obviously the retort didn't make sense to him. How could he be a "Yid" when his papa was an NKVD official? It was probably his papa who'd told him about Latvian exiles. I was often taunted with the phrase, "Yid, sitting on a mud fence," though I didn't know exactly what a "Yid" was. I was teased in school, too, because I was the smallest and as skinny as the orphans. It didn't look as if I were going to acquire those beautiful curves of which Lyusya was so proud. Several times, she showed me the mounds they call breasts. After careful study, I concluded it was unlikely I'd ever grow into a blooming young girl from such a bony one, and that life was therefore not worth living. My knees, elbows, ribs—everything about me stuck out.

Sister caused me her share of unhappiness, too. She was only slightly taller, but round, rosy, and beautiful. Why, I can't understand. She ate the same things, except that she didn't get sick on fodder soup, and she had a quieter disposition. I used to fret a great deal about everything, and Mama, trying to reason with me, would say, "That's why you're so thin and blue, one can see right through you, you slip away like quicksilver. No face, no body, just eyes. How do you keep body and soul together?"

My soul was apparently firmly attached. Not once

did I fall sick, even after the time they found me on
the ice. I never coughed and didn't even catch a cold
in all six years of my first stay in Siberia. But from time
to time, I'd roll my eyes, clear my throat, cough, and
swallow convulsively the way I used to as a child back
home to show Mama my throat hurt. That was when
I really wanted some hot milk desperately.

My sister and I both did well in school, even though
we had to do our homework at recess or go to one of
our classmates' houses in the evenings because neither
of us had any textbooks. I liked singing, drawing, reading,
and history best. We had the same teacher for all subjects.
She was always apprehensive when she called me to
the blackboard. I'd announce the subject of the lesson
loudly and then go off into fantasy. It must have made
some sense, however, because the children sometimes
asked the teacher to let me finish.

Most of the exiles we knew had strange, non-Russian
surnames. Therefore, when the teacher told us to ink
out the pictures and names of certain men in our history
text, many of whom had non-Russian names, like
Blücher, Yakir, and Tukhachevsky, I assumed they had
been exiled for something or other, too. We loved dipping
our fingers in the inkwell filled with diluted soot and
were sometimes overzealous. I once inked out Comrade
Kaganovich himself because his name sounded like an
"exiled" one to me. I was lucky I was only eleven years
old.

Papa's brother visited us once again in the summer
of 1944. It is incredible that he managed. The war was
still going on, train tickets weren't to be had, the trains
had no timetable, and he had a job, besides. Again he
brought us paper, pencils, and some money, and he took
my sister back to Moscow with him. He wanted very
much to see Papa, but visits weren't allowed.

Papa got permission to receive one package a year.

We'd save up sugar for him for a long time and buy a little tobacco. Sometimes we even managed to get a pack of cigarettes by barter, and Mama would keep that for the package, too. Once someone managed to bring us a letter from him that wasn't the usual camp letter. Because of the censorship, most of his letters told us little, but this time he wrote he was not far from Krasnoyarsk, in a camp called Kraslag; that the article under which he was sentenced was number 58, section 10; that he had been sentenced by the *troika* in Dzerzhinsk to ten years; and that after finishing his term in camp, he would still be subject to exile and deprivation of rights for life. He also wrote that he thought about us constantly, loved us very much, and told us we should not lose hope, he would hold out somehow.

Things were a little easier for Mama and me after my sister left, but, for some reason, all the exiles were dying to go to the city, and Mama was possessed by the idea, too. The closest city—west of us, of course—was Kansk, near which they had put us off the train that night three years before. My uncle had advised Mama to move closer to the center, too, so she began working at it. She got medical certificates, became very agitated, even cried at times, and often bawled me out for nothing. It took her a whole year.

Then came the day of victory, the ninth of May, 1945. Our school took part in the parade, and I carried a drum in front of the whole school. I always beat the drums for lessons on military matters and at Pioneer meetings. I hadn't lost my feeling for rhythm.

There were heartaches after the war was over, too. The woman who rented to us had two sons at the front, the younger one mobilized at the very end of the war. She was expecting them, making preparations for the reunion, but instead she got two death notices. It took Mama a long time to calm her; she wanted to do away with herself.

Then we got permission to move to Kansk, and in July, 1945, when I had completed fifth grade, we left Dzerzhinsk.

KANSK

Mama rented a minuscule room, and again there were four of us living together. Mama's friend Musya had come with us from Dzerzhinsk, and my sister had returned from Moscow after studying a year there. As always, Mama and I slept in one bed behind the stove, with Musya's bed close by, while Sister made herself a place to sleep at night by moving the table and stool into the corner. It was always dark in our room, as the two little windows at ground level let in no light, but all you had to do was flick the switch to have electric light. That astounded me. I'd forgotten many things during our four years in Siberia. You didn't have to clean the glass of the kerosene lamp every day anymore, trembling with fear it might break and you couldn't buy a new one. You no longer had to stand for hours in long lines when the kerosene arrived. You didn't have to get dirty cutting the smoking wick—just flick a switch. That alone was reason enough to fall in love with Kansk. And on the whole, everything about the city was solid, even the name of our street: Red Army Street, house 99—though that wasn't really our house, but that of our landlady, Praskovya Ivanovna, which we immediately shortened to Aproksya. Our little house looked terrible from the outside, half hut, half ruin, with holes in the roof, warped doors, and windows half boarded up with plywood.

Kansk was a big town. There were several grammar schools, a real movie theater, a post office, a hospital, a market, a huge textile combine beyond the River Kan, and several stores, one of which proudly bore the reliable

inscription "Univermag," or supermarket. In the center
of town was a large open square into which many streets
flowed. None was asphalted or paved. It was sometimes
impossible to cross the road after a rain, even in rubber
boots.

Getting water was much simpler here; there were lots
of pumps in the street. Until then, I'd thought water
was found only in wells. Here, all you had to do was
pump, and it poured out. Of course you had to walk
two blocks to fetch it, but we bought a yoke and I soon
learned to carry two full pails without a spill, though
I staggered like a drunk to do it.

My sister had changed a great deal in a year. She
had grown up and joined the Komsomol, the Communist
youth organization. She treated me disdainfully and
arrogantly. She loved telling about Moscow, with which
she was in love, and she was obviously bored in Kansk.
She had lived with our uncle in the very center of
Moscow, near the General Post Office on Kirov Street.
Almost every sentence she uttered began, "In Moscow,
we . . ."

"Why didn't you stay in Moscow?"

"That's none of your business."

"Then don't put on airs."

"You're just a country bumpkin, one shouldn't have
anything to do with you."

Sometimes, just to annoy her, I'd ask in an innocent
tone, "Did you have electricity in Moscow?"

"Electricity? I'll say we did, you numbskull. Do you
know what a trolleybus is? Of course not. Can you picture
a subway? Of course not. They're always building beautiful new subway lines in Moscow, the best architects in
the capital design them. You'd 'Oh' and 'Ah' over the
wonderful stations with gold everywhere, elegant chan-
deliers, mosaics, marble. You and your electricity! I bet
you've already forgotten what a streetcar looks like. By

the way, they're going to take streetcars out here and there in the overall plan for reconstructing Moscow."

"Why?"

"Not modern enough."

"And how did you get to be so well informed?"

"Not everyone's an ignoramus like you. You're politically completely illiterate, while I'm a Komsomolka."

"I'm going to join the Komsomol soon, too."

"*You?* Ha, ha, ha, who needs you there? The Komsomol needs real people, not nincompoops like you. Besides, you'll just have to wait patiently another two years like a good girl."

"So what? As for you, the whole time you were in Moscow they had to worry about your getting yourself in trouble with some boy."

Sister turned red as a lobster and lost her temper.

"You're a complete idiot. Where'd you get that idea? And where'd you get such a nasty tongue, anyway?"

"I read Uncle's letters. And Aunty's. Mama called them 'rigamarole' letters and dreaded them. They complained about you all the time. They wrote that when you were allowed out until seven, you'd show up, unconcerned, at eight. And that more than once they found some pretty suspicious letters of yours."

"The fools," Sister sputtered.

"And that you'd already gotten yourself a boyfriend, and God alone knows what you and he did together. And that they had to worry all the time for fear you'd get yourself in trouble with him."

"You're an idiot. And they're fools. Mama's a fool, too, to show you such idiotic letters."

"And you're a fool if you think Mama showed them to me. She hid them and I found them."

Unpleasant conversations are usually broken off by whoever finds them the most disagreeable. Sister said haughtily, "Run and get water, and make it quick, don't dawdle on the way like yesterday. And peel the potatoes.

Get some firewood, not just whatever's on top, pick out the driest. And chop some kindling, the wood's all damp. Get moving, don't just stand there with your mouth hanging open. Mama'll be home from work soon and you haven't done a thing. I'll start the stove meantime."

"Bah, smartie. Perhaps you want me to tickle you under your arms, or scratch your feet? Let's see you pick up your feet. I'll bring the water and peel the potatoes, you fetch the wood and chop the kindling yourself. You've been skipping around Moscow on subways and stupid trolleybuses while I've spent my life chopping kindling and running my legs off. My fingers are worn to stumps from chopping kindling. I don't have a normal one left."

"Do as you're told."

"I won't. And don't yell at me. Just because you're older doesn't mean you're smarter."

I used to drive her into a fury, and she had the same effect on me. She was plump, rosy, with a luxuriant bosom I was embarrassed to look at but secretly envied. She had brought back some old dresses. No one thought it necessary to make her threadbare jumpers over for me, and I swam in them.

"Mama, tell me, why are you afraid of going *there?*"

"None of your business."

"Mamochka, it's funny how a day or two before your appointment comes up, you start grumbling at us, finding fault with everything, and when the time comes to go, you put on your awful sackcloth skirt and pluck tufts of wool out of your already threadbare, ragged sweater so they stick out, and wipe off your lipstick. Why?"

"Stick to your own affairs and stop pestering me with stupid questions."

"They're not stupid and you know it and just don't want to say. But at least tell me then why we're exiles?"

"Will you leave me alone, you naughty child? Why

do you suddenly want to know everything? You're getting a little too curious. The less you know, the better. You start chattering and the next thing you know, you'll catch it."

"What do you mean?"

"You'll get sent up north."

"Why?"

"Why, for your stupid chatter."

"Then do we have to keep still all the time?"

"It would be a good idea."

"Then I want to know. And who am I supposed to ask besides you?"

"Oh Lord, I still can't answer you."

"But nobody else knows."

"Have you asked anybody else?"

"Haven't I though! Falya's mama doesn't know why you have to go register, and Falya doesn't even know what the NKVD is. So tell me why."

"Because we're exiles. And exiles have to be checked up on to make sure they don't run away. That's why all exiles have to go register every two weeks."

"Do they run away?"

"I don't know. Stop chattering and do your homework."

"Mamochka, one last question. Why did they arrest Papa?"

"I don't know. That's the way it had to be. And if you don't stop now, I'll take your book away and you won't get anything to eat."

Dilemmas arose and there was no one to explain them. I couldn't figure them out by myself. For instance, we had to fill out questionnaires in school. All the other children knew what to write, but I'd sit there struggling. In column such-and-such, Mama had told me to write so-and-so, and to certain questions I was to give completely false and incomprehensible answers. For instance,

I'd write "died on the workers' front" about Papa, though I knew he was in prison. Why? "That's the way it has to be," Mama would say. Or, for social origin, I'd write "Employees," though I knew we were the most unregenerate, unadulterated, big-bellied bourgeois, not employees at all.

When I wrote "Jewish" in the column labeled "nationality," the child next to me whistled rather strangely and said, "So you're a Yid on top of everything else?"

"On top of what?"

"Why, being exiles. You're really all over the place."

There were a great many exiles in Kansk, from Latvia, Lithuania, Estonia, the western Ukraine and Byelorussia, and from somewhere in Moldavia. There were many Volga Germans and Tartars. There were recent exiles and exiles from way back. There were Poles, Ukrainians, even some Chinese. And we heard there was a huge prison camp near Kansk called Kanlag. The children got to know about one another from their parents; the parents got to know each other standing in line to register. Somehow this brought both parents and children closer together.

The women sometimes gathered in our hut in the evenings. First they'd have the usual tedious exchange about who'd found something to eat and where. Each would boast of her success in finding something, and then they'd start talking about their husbands. Some knew nothing about their men, some got letters. Many of the men had been shot and some had died in camp of hunger. One wrote he'd like to embrace his dearest and best beloved before he died, but that there was no chance of it. The women often cried. Then they'd begin a boring conversation about their children.

"You know, Zhenya, my Lev's gotten completely out of hand. He's not a child, he's a savage. Did we ever dream our children would turn out like this? You know, it's a sin to say it, but I sometimes think my husband's better off not to have lived to see this, though dying in camp isn't the best fate either. But what would he say if he saw my little rascal now? The little devil actually hits me. And to think my husband was planning to send Lev to England to study banking."

My Mamochka usually put in her say, too.

"For days, my youngest has been coming and asking what a hustler is. What can you tell a child? I'm not quite sure myself, and I can't get it off that child's mind. She drives me crazy with her questions. The instant I get home from work, I hear her 'Why, why, why?' And she often gets me in a corner, I don't know what to tell her. Both of them have gotten so rude, it's awful. They yell at each other, they've fought a few times. At least the older one's busy with community activities and does her homework, she's a studious child, but the younger one is out on the streets all day and won't listen to her older sister. She keeps saying it's because age is no sign of intelligence or strength. Where does a child get these ideas? There's no settling her down to do her homework, everything comes easy to her, her teachers are always complaining. You know, I'm ashamed to say it, but she had a *three* in conduct in Dzerzhinsk. I'm afraid to think what she'll do next. This isn't the kind of future my husband planned for us either, he was going to send both of them to Paris for a few years to study languages."

They thought I was asleep, that's why Mamochka talked so frankly. Actually, I was lying in bed with the covers over my head. How cleverly I'd fooled Mama. I'd gotten a new passion recently—books. It wasn't true that I was out on the streets all day. Sometimes I even skipped school in order to sit somewhere and read. I read everything that came my way, even scientific works. At the time, I'd read Feuchtwanger, Dreiser, Balzac, and

De Maupassant, not to mention Tolstoi, Gogol, and Chekhov.

But the books that made the greatest impression on me weren't the ones you could get in school or the ones Mama brought home and gave us to read; they were the ones she carefully hid from us. They were called "boulevard literature" and were published in Riga. All of them had shameless covers—almost naked beauties, sometimes behind bars, sometimes on couches, sometimes with fully and correctly dressed young men. My heart would stop beating when I looked at these covers. We were forbidden to touch them, supposedly because we didn't know how to treat books and bent back the corners. All of these books were terribly tattered, glued and reglued; sometimes Mama even brought them home piece by piece. The way she tried to hide them! I think we'd have found them if she'd put them down a well, but she sometimes simply hid them under her pillow. Mama obviously underestimated us. We'd often fight right in front of her over who would be the first to read those forbidden books.

There was a kind of flea market in Kansk where you could buy a flashlight with batteries for a certain amount of rags, bones, or scrap metal. Because I needed a lot of batteries and we didn't have rags and bones in our house, I used to poke about in other people's courtyards collecting scrap iron. They gave you more for that. The market didn't pay money, but you could get things you couldn't buy for any kind of money, like colored embroidery threads or scissors or a wide garter to keep stockings from falling down. I got a flashlight with batteries, and I'd go to bed early like a good girl, cover up my head, and light up the breathtaking lines with my flashlight. I used to become faint with terror and excitement reading the books of Kryzhanovska and Princess Olga Bebutova, but it was Verbitska's heroes in *Keys to Happiness* that brought me my greatest suffering and delight. The heroine was called Manya. I was often Manya.

Our miserable room was so tiny it was hard to take a step in it without bumping into something. Inspired by *Keys to Happiness,* trembling with excitement, naked, with our only kitchen towel thrown over my shoulders, I danced as "she" had for "him." I would literally have died with shame if anyone had caught me doing it.

Mother got herself a job as knitter for a *promartel;* a producer's cooperative of artisans. Sometimes they gave her work to take home—thick socks, mittens, and shawls. I learned to knit when I was ten, and Sister and I used to help her. Later on, this was a great asset to us. If we had an order, she and I could make a sweater or a woman's jacket in one night. This saved us from hunger more than once in our student years.

One of the most important events in our lives was the Sunday secondhand market. Anything that might be of the slightest use was sold there, though it was often hard to see what use something might be. Mother became a master at bargaining and selling tattered old remnants.

"How much are you asking for this rag?" a woman would ask carelessly.

"What do you mean, rag—that's a magnificent foreign jacket, pure wool. Five hundred, and that's a gift," Mama would reply indignantly.

"You've lost your mind, woman, five hundred for that piece of junk? Make it half that."

"Four hundred and fifty, and only for you because you appreciate good things."

"Are you crazy? It's full of holes, and for two-fifty, you can buy half a sack of potatoes."

Mother would come down a little. "Three-fifty and not a kopeck less."

They'd agree on half a sack of potatoes, some frozen

milk, and a head of cabbage. Each thought she had cleverly outwitted the other.

"Oi, it's killing, that was real rubbish. I wore it, the children wore it, you could hardly save the yarn from it, it was going to pieces in her hands, a mass of knots! Oi, I can't stand it, I was afraid my pure wool jacket would fall apart in that fool's hands. And now we have potatoes for a week," Mama boasted.

Potatoes were our basic food. We loved them every way, but most of all simply boiled with sauerkraut and a tiny bit of butter. It was a holiday when Mama let us cook all the potatoes we wanted.

We still had ration cards. The bread cards allowed us bread every other day, still bitter-tasting and heavy as loam, but the ration was bigger and the waiting lines less terrible. Sometimes Mama had enough time to get our "brick" after work. Once Mama lost our bread ration cards and for about two weeks couldn't get bread for any kind of money. Selling bread in the market was strictly forbidden because it was stolen anywhere and everywhere, beginning in the bakery and ending at the stores. You could get ten years for selling bread.

There were meat cards, fat cards, and sugar cards, too. For meat, we were sometimes issued a bit of not very fresh-smelling fish, usually humpback salmon, salted or half smoked. We'd eat our month's ration in one sitting with potatoes and bread. I think we got a kilogram of fish for the three of us per month. I can't remember their issuing meat once. On our fat cards, we sometimes got about half a kilo of lard or vegetable oil, and as for sugar, either they'd issue nothing for a whole month or we'd get a few candies glued together like a rock. Lump sugar, which we'd break into little bits with an ax, was given out only for the holidays of the Seventh of November and the First of May.

On the whole, we lived in a quite civilized manner

in Kansk. Mama even managed to get some plates some-where. With individual plates came equal rights, whereas before, since I was the smallest, I got the least—that was when we were still eating out of one bowl in Mokry-Elnik and Dzerzhinsk. In those days Mama had often banged our foreheads with a spoon for waging a "socialist com-petition" to see who ate the fastest.

There was absolutely no time to think; you always had to be doing something. All day long, all I heard was, "Bring water," "Wash the floor," "Take out . . . Bring in . . ." From time to time, I was sent to stand in line or to someone's house to fetch something. I some-times had homework to do, too, and I was always wanting to read. As for thinking, there was absolutely no time. The only peaceful place was the outhouse. It wasn't easy to get me out of there.

The outhouse was not far from our hut and quite decent—you could even go there in winter. It stood in a corner of the courtyard and had a door that hooked shut and a tiny little window. In the middle was a platform you had to climb up on, which was a little hard for me because I was so short, and squatting wasn't very com-fortable either. But I even managed to read in this squat-ting position, which made the landlady complain to Mama. Besides the four of us, she had three other families living in her tiny three-room house, and they sometimes wanted to use the privy, too. It was a somewhat limited pleasure, of course. The air was stale, the cesspool rarely cleaned, and in summer, it was swarming with big green flies and crawling with worms. The cesspool was sup-posed to be covered with a plank, but seldom was.

Beautiful fantasies used to come into my head there. I was grown-up and gorgeous, with languorous eyes and curls like Shirley Temple. I was in Paris. I had a separate room no one had the right to enter, where I could do what I pleased. No one made me wash in ice-cold water. I didn't have to saw and chop wood, I didn't have to stoke the stove, yet the room was very warm somehow. Occupying first place in my fantasy was a dressing table like the one Mama once had, with quantities of jars, vials, tubes, and pretty flagons. And, of course, a powder box with its downy puff.

I slowly draw on silk stockings and make sure the seams are straight. Then I pick out some shoes, of which I have a whole battery, all with the thinnest possible heels. With lazy grace, I run a handsome brush through the curls that fall in luxurious waves over my bare shoulders. I spray myself with French perfume—Coty—out of a crystal flagon with a yellow rubber bulb covered with network. I glance at my minuscule watch. I'm expecting "him."

At this point, my fantasy usually broke off because I couldn't visualize clearly what "he" was there for. But it was all beautiful, and my heart beat fast.

One day my daydreams were interrupted by a child crying in the house next door, where there was a day nursery. The fence was broken down, and the walls of our outhouse had fairly wide cracks, so you could look into the neighbors' courtyard without interrupting your business. I saw a group of puppies running there.

"Splash!" I caught a glimpse of a black, hairy little ball flashing below me. Something was floundering in the cesspool. I swept into action. The first tool I saw was a pitchfork. I grabbed it and fished the "something" out of the cesspool. It was no longer black and fluffy, it was pitiful and whining—but alive. How happy I was!

This was Jack. In honor of Jack London, whom I adored at that time. Lord, I had so much to do before Mama got home—wash and dry Jack, think up a pack of lies, and in general prepare myself morally.

Mama had hardly entered the room when she

wrinkled her nose. She looked at me suspiciously. Like a good little girl, I was doing my homework. With good humor. Even more suspicious.

"What smells?"

"Smells where, Mamochka?"

"In the room."

"Why, Mama, it can't smell, look—I even washed the floor, look, it's still damp, look, I'm doing my homework."

"Why did you suddenly wash the floor today?"

"It looked dirty to me. Do you want to eat?"

"Of course. But will you tell me now what smells so?"

"You're just imagining it smells. Maybe they came to clean the privy? Yes, of course, I saw a man there with that smelly boy."

"Child, I can see by your eyes you're lying. Besides, there's no smell in the street."

Mama went behind the stove to change clothes. There, on our bed, wrapped in our only kitchen towel, lay Jack, shivering because I hadn't had time to heat the water and had washed him in cold.

I managed to jump behind the stove before Mama got there and started to help her change.

"My God, what's that?"

"Mama, that's Jack," I said sturdily.

"Who?"

"Jack. My Jack. Our Jack."

"Whose?"

"Mamochka, he's so wonderful, he's a darling, you'll see yourself when we can unwrap him. He's all black with a white chest and paws, and Mama, just think, the tip of his tail is white, too."

"Stop that chatter. And take him out, right now. All we need in the house is a dog, there's no room for us to turn around in ourselves and nothing to eat. Lord in heaven! My only towel! You naughty child! I scraped to get it, I don't have anything to dry the dishes with, and this good-for-nothing takes it to play tricks with. Out, and don't set foot here again. March!"

I picked up Jack from the bed and unwrapped him. He trembled. And stank. Mama was right, but he had such trusting brown eyes, he looked at me with such love, and his nose was wet, and he was all black with white paws.

"All right, Mama, we're going."

"Make it snappy and don't set foot here again. We'll have to give the place a good airing."

I put my coat on without letting Jack out of my arms.

"Where are you going?"

"You said we should go."

"I asked you, where are you going?"

"I'm going with Jack."

"Heavens above, it's a wonder this dreadful child hasn't driven me to the grave yet. What am I to do with her?"

"Let Jack stay."

"Not under any condition. Don't we have fleas enough from your cat? You don't think a dog's going to catch mice and birds to feed itself, do you? You have to feed a dog."

"I know. But Mamochka, just think, if we both have to catch mice and birds, we could die of hunger and cold. Where are we going to live? Who'll take us in, little as we are?"

We were already in the doorway. From there, Jack hardly smelled.

"Will you tell me why your Jack smells so?"

"Hurrah! My Jack! Mamochka darling, I'll tell you everything, just don't get angry."

"What am I to do with this curse of a child?"

"Let Jack stay, like Jack, keep Jack."

"All right. But now you listen to me. In the house, no. And you'll have to talk to the landlady, she doesn't like dogs. And if I once see you not doing your lessons and playing with Jack instead, he flies right out. And please don't think I gave in because you used blackmail."

"Used what?"

"Blackmail. That's when someone acts the way you did."

"Hurrah, Momochka, I'll do everything you tell me and not use blackmail."

"Fine. Now settle this stinkpot somewhere and let's air the room."

From then on, we were six—the four of us, the cat Yuki, and my beloved Jack. Yuki was more often than not out hunting during the day, but slept at my feet at night. Jack, on the other hand, was at home only during the day when Mama was at work and slept in the passageway at night at first. Later, my sister and I set up a box for him near the entrance. He grew up to be not very big, but handsome, well-behaved, and playful. He wasn't a pure-bred spaniel like Sherry; he was more of a Siberian husky, if you looked at him closely. Mama came to love him, too, though she often b-l-a-c-k-m-a-i-l-e-d me over Jack.

Life was harder for Mama than for us, of course—problems, one after the other from morning until night. One problem was our felt boots. They cost a lot, we were growing out of them, and to have them fixed was a whole rigamarole. While they were being fixed, we'd have nothing to wear, and it was impossible to go out even when it was only fifteen degrees below zero without felt shoes. It was simpler in summer—we went barefoot. But we had to be dressed and wear shoes to go to school. We were growing out of our clothes, too. I wore sister's cast-offs, but she (how embarrassing it was) even had to order brassieres. Nor was the matter of getting enough food easy. Once again, we were saved by the packages Mama's sister in Palestine sent us. She used to send wool jackets, suits, and shoes. One such package every six months was all we needed.

Mama developed a permanent clientele. Her steady customers were wives of officers from the military base, wives of officials from Kanlag, store clerks, and a few others who stole here and there and resold things. Sometimes these ladies came to look at things in our house. We always scrubbed the floor and washed the curtains for their coming, but they rarely sat down, usually bargaining standing up. If the bargaining was successful, we'd go with Mama to the military base or elsewhere, where they'd hand over the goods we'd gotten in barter: flour, potatoes, salt herring, sometimes butter, and sometimes half jars of American canned sausage. That was absolutely indescribably good. Sometimes Mama managed to get a bundle of coarse tobacco into the bargain. Smoking was really the only problem that affected her alone, though here, too, we took part. She managed to get tobacco stalks cheaply somewhere and dry them and we would help crumble them. They gave off a strong, acrid smoke, but Mama, rolling a thick cigarette out of newsprint, enjoyed the puffing that ended in coughing. What she didn't think up to get hold of tobacco! She even tried growing it herself, but the weather was too cold. She bartered things for tobacco, begged for tobacco, sometimes even sold her share of bread for it. And she still had to buy newspapers for cigarette paper besides. God help us if we snatched a piece of newspaper for more prosaic uses. Back in Dzerzhinsk, Mama taught us to use burdock and other leaves from shade trees that grew around outhouses. We didn't know what toilet paper was. Mama always grumbled, "Is it too much work for you to pick leaves, you princesses? Don't you dare take my newspaper!"

Our family must have been born under a lucky star. Good fortune often smiled on us. Once a nephew of Father's unexpectedly appeared. In the winter of 1946, he suddenly sent a telegram to say he was coming through Kansk. The train passed through at night. Faint with fear, at night, in bitter cold, Mama and I raced to the station, three kilometers from home. All sorts of bands roved the city at that time, the "Black Cats," "Red Cats," all sorts of "dogs"—in other words, lots of robbers and thieves. A number of penal army units were billeted there, too, and they also committed crimes. There was constant talk of someone being killed here or robbed there. We ran fast, looking around constantly. If a figure loomed up in the distance, we'd freeze like two dogs pointing, fade into the wall, wait for the figure to disappear, then run on, teeth chattering. The train was late, the station was closed. Stiff with cold, Mama and I rubbed each other's whitening noses and cheeks and hopped about like two rabbits.

Then the troop train pulled in. The half-open, heated cargo wagons, giving off sounds of laughter, singing, and harmonica playing, crawled slowly past us. Mama and I were the only people on the whole platform. The soldiers called to us from the cars, inviting us to come along. Mama looked around fearfully. But then, in the open door of one of the cars, Papa's nephew appeared, shouted to us cheerily that he had won the war, beaten the Germans and Japanese, and was going home to Riga to change his military uniform for civilian clothes. It seemed to me everyone in the train was drunk, Papa's nephew, too. He had time to add that his mother, Papa's sister, had been killed by the Germans and his aunt, Father's second sister, too. When the train had already started moving, packages flew down at us. I ran alongside his car a bit, and he took off his watch and gave it to me.

The packages contained yards of wonderful silk that Mama sold very successfully on the military base. She bartered the watch very profitably, too.

The following day, I felt almost equal with everyone in school for the first time when, with apparent casualness, though bursting with pride, I told how we had met our cousin that night, an officer, whose uniform was so becoming to him it was a pity he would be changing into civilian dress after all those heroic years at the front. At home, too, we talked only of how lucky we were. We even felt it awkward that some should be showered with such good fortune while others never had any luck. Mama sang and indulged us; Jack and I raced one another, barking; and in the evening, we had tea with homemade cake made with almost pure white flour and powdered eggs. Mama even had me take a piece of cake to an old woman, who had no one even to give her some tea, let alone a wristwatch, as mother stressed.

I had become friends with Galya Vladimirova, an intelligent, pretty girl with green eyes. The family had a big red-brick house with sturdy shutters, a high fence, and a very mean dog on a chain who was let loose at night. There were lace curtains at the windows, not gauze ones like ours. Except with Galya and one other girl in my class, I never got farther than the kitchen of any house in all the time we lived in Kansk. Everyone there lived behind high fences, kept mean dogs on chains, hung locks on the gate, and closed the shutters quite early in the evening. The people weren't as friendly as even those in Dzerzhinsk, not to speak of Mokry-Elnik. There, they'd given us presents and milk when we came, there were no fences, and they used to visit us, to sit in the evenings and talk with Mama. Here, except for other exiles, no one came to see us and no one invited Mama either.

I'd never seen so many drunks before. Around the market, near the beer stall, even when there wasn't any beer, women as well as men lolled about dead drunk, especially on market days. There were often fights and shouts of abuse in the market itself. And they stole brazenly, snatching things right out of your hands if you didn't watch. Also, when I'd gone to fetch milk in the village or in Dzerzhinsk, they'd always pour me a little extra so I could drink two or three swallows. Here, all the old women's hands shook, spilling milk back in the can after it was measured. Mama often asked me how much I'd drunk, but I never touched it, it was just that the sellers were greedy.

I was always a bit intimidated by Galya's house. It was very clean, there were porcelain statuettes around, and the toilet was right next to the house, you only had to go out into the passageway. They had a clever device for washing, too, a kind of washstand, but you didn't have to pour water out of a jug as at our house, it came by itself. It was only in Kansk that we acquired a washstand. Before, we had simply poured water on each other's hands or collected it from the jug in our mouths and then spat it out over our hands. That's why I hated washing myself in winter. The icy water made my teeth ache, but Mama forced me to wash every morning.

Sister did socially useful work. She was an activist. She went to general Komsomol meetings, to meetings of the VLKSM Committee (Leninist Young Communist League of the Soviet Union), to which she had been elected, and on Sundays she went to collect scrap metal. To my satisfaction, she was seldom home.

There was less that two years' difference between us, but compared to me, she and her classmates were serious and grown-up. They had lots of secrets and usually whispered when I was around. My sister had found a boyfriend here, too. I liked him very much, but tried to keep out of his sight. He didn't consider me a person. He used to flick me on the nose, pull my braids, and generally make fun of me. It wasn't surprising. My sister was so splendid and serious while I was a scarecrow, restless, overexcitable, inquisitive, and flat as a board.

I swore a thousand solemn oaths to stop making faces, whistling with four fingers, fighting with little boys, playing leapfrog and tipcat; to stop jumping around like a billygoat and learn to walk gracefully—in short, to become as splendid and serious as my sister. I even studied how to roll my eyes the way she did to express contempt. I wanted to take my homework seriously, too. Sister and her boyfriend used to get together in the hayloft to prepare for lessons and exams, but it seems I got in their way. Sometimes she told me what a contemptible creature I was: "It's every Komsomol's duty to study hard."

I agreed with her. What I didn't like was that Komsomols had too many of these duties. Digging potatoes on kolkhozes was a duty, voluntary work on Sundays was a duty, perfect attendance at school another duty, participating in clubs—also a duty. Even singing in the choir was a duty. Sister was proud of all this. I annoyed her.

"Who do you take after to turn out such a fool?"

"You, except you got all the flesh."

"How can the earth bear you?"

"Bearing me's nothing, I'm thin, but why you don't sink right through the ground, I don't understand."

"I'd just like to know what you'll be when you grow up. A furnace stoker, probably, though I wouldn't trust you with a shovel. She doesn't want to study, you ask her to go get something—she doesn't want to, ask her not to make noise—she doesn't want to. Forever underfoot. And don't you dare spy on me, don't sneak up and watch while we're doing lessons in the hayloft. If I catch you once more, I'll tell Mama."

"And I'll tell her what you're doing."

"Idiot! And if you stick your nose in our classroom once more, I'll fix it for you. Do you think I don't know on whose account you follow us around? You don't think they want any part of you, do you?"

I turned red and fell silent. How had she guessed? *They* were the twin boys in her class, Zhenya and Volodya. It was true I was attracted to them though I couldn't tell one from the other (later this seemed very simple). They lived on the other side of the river in the houses belonging to the textile combine. I'd heard all sorts of gossip at home about their mother, how she had "taken up with" an engineer in the combine, after the boys' father had "disappeared" somewhere. Mama used to condemn her, pursing her lips and saying, "Of course, it isn't easy to remain an honest woman with two little children on your hands."

My sister wasn't right at all in saying they hadn't noticed me. One of them—Volodya, I think—even danced with me when the older classmates had a party I managed to sneak into. That was the first time I'd danced with a boy in my life, at a time when girls almost always danced with each other. Only couples who had started going together danced together, boy with girl. I burned with embarrassment and pride.

School evening parties were great events. They always began with a lecture, by someone from the regional Party committee, usually about the international situation, which lasted an hour and a half. You had to attend or they wouldn't let you go to the party. The doors were locked shut at the very beginning of the lecture. Afterward, there was an amateur concert: a choir sang, verses were read, and soloists sang. I volunteered for the choir only to have a chance of worming my way into the party. I had no voice, but it wasn't particularly called for because we mostly sang songs about Stalin, and what counted was singing as loudly as possible. There was no school auditorium, so everything was set up in the hallway, where it was rather dark and very cold. People usually sat in their coats and scarves with felt boots on their feet. Then the tables and benches would be moved out, the responsible Komsomol would wind up the gramophone, and the dance would begin. For parties celebrating the First of May and Seventh of November, an accordionist was invited.

My heart leaped into my throat and stayed there when, at the very first dance of my life, first Volodya, then Zhenya, asked me to dance. They played a fox-trot—"Lizanka, I asked you a serious question, do you love me or noo-oo-ot?" sang the gramophone. One step forward, one to the side, one step forward, one to the side. My feet wouldn't move, my arms were wooden and trembling, and my only thought was, "Oh Lord, if I can just avoid tripping over him and falling down." I got through the evening. It seems I was with Volodya then. He took me home, and for the first time, I regretted we lived so close to school. I felt I was falling in love, and from then on, I had no trouble telling the twins apart, though they were so alike they fooled everyone.

I met Volodya a few years later in Moscow. He was studying at the Institute, as was Zhenya. But there was still a marked difference between them—Volodya had dared to assert his origins by changing his name and patronymic to Jewish ones. It seems his mother divorced his father when the latter was arrested, married that engineer in Kansk, and changed even the sons' surnames for very Russian ones. Zhenya kept his name, but Volodya became Vladimir Kornfeld.

When I was thirteen, back in Kansk, Volodya often

took me home. We'd walk past the NKVD building where Mama was so afraid of going. At the time, I took no notice of it. It was only a few years later, when I was carried half dead from that building, that I mechanically observed how close it was to my old school.

Sister cursed the day she gave me a recommendation to join the Komsomol, where I was accepted through some kind of pull, because I was only thirteen and members of the VLKSM were supposed to be fourteen. She sincerely believed people like me should be shot. I used to annoy her terribly.

"If you're such a great Communist, tell me what the 'principle of democratic centralism' is," I'd challenge her. The principle didn't interest me at all, but to join, I had to learn the *Regulations of the VLKSM* by heart from cover to cover.

She would patiently repeat word for word what was written in the *Regulations*.

"But what does it mean: 'electivity from below upward and responsibility from above downward'? However you slice it, I don't get it, but it's got to have some sort of sense," I insisted.

"It does, but not to birdbrains like you."

"All right, then use your powerful mind to explain it to me. What's a principle?"

"A principle is something everyone has to have. All Communists are people of principles. For example, they live by the Socialist principle 'From each according to his capacity, to each according to his labor.' Got it?"

"No. With all your capacities, you've just confused me more than ever with your 'to each, from each.' And what's this here—'Everyone is equal'?"

"How stupid you are. Everyone's equal in our country. You ask such silly questions. What's unclear about that?"

"Are we equal, too?"

"Of course!"

"Then why do we live in this repulsive hut where we have to study on the bed while Galya Vladimirova lives in a brick house with a brick wall around it? And why did that wretch Leva drop out of school because he had nothing to wear and his papa died in camp, while your handsome Volodya Kolomitsev walks around in real calf-leather shoes because *his* papa is a government procurator? And why are we always being threatened with being sent north? Aha, I've got you, you don't have a thing to say!"

"I do, but it's best to have nothing to do with a snake in the grass like you."

I joined the VLKSM and parroted the words about Komsomol duties and all sorts of principles glibly, but I didn't want to stay in Kansk, especially since both Volodya and Zhenya were leaving for Moscow. Suddenly we heard rumors that the children of exiles who had died or were in prison were being rounded up in Siberia by the Red Cross of the Baltic republics and sent to orphanages in those republics or to relatives, if the relatives would accept them. Children up to the age of sixteen were eligible. I fit the requirements: Papa was in prison and I had relatives. All we had to find out was whether the relatives would accept "that kind of child." Mama was sure Papa's brother in Moscow had given up after his unsuccessful experience with my smart little sister. We had still another relative, Mama's sister in Kaunas. I tried to persuade Mama to let me go. Once there, I'd be able to make an impression on my relatives and they wouldn't be able to send me back.

"If you don't let me go peacefully, I'll run away or hang myself."

"No rope could hold you," Mama said, passing it off as a joke.

"That's because you're always pestering me with lectures."

"Do you think you know everything without being told?"

"No, but I often react out of spite because all day all I hear is that I'm an idiot, stick my nose in things that aren't my business, don't walk right, don't talk right, and you even complain I don't sleep like a human being and keep kicking you. So I want to sleep alone. Let me go, please."

We exchanged letters with my relatives. My aunt in Kaunas immediately agreed to take me; my uncle in Moscow set a few moral conditions. I was more tempted by Moscow; I agreed to the moral conditions. But while the correspondence was going on, the Red Cross mission came to an end. It seems Mama had known about the mission from the start, but hadn't dreamed of letting me go. Now we had to look for some other way of sending me. NKVD permission wasn't necessary because I came under the category of free people and, besides, children weren't listed on the special register.

This time, too, fortune smiled on me. One of our former neighbors, also an exile, unexpectedly arrived from Dzerzhinsk with her son. Thanks to some powerful influence her sister enjoyed, she had gotten permission to take her son to her sister's in Riga herself. We decided I would go along with them to Moscow. But when they were sent train tickets, there was none for me, and the chances of getting a ticket in Kansk for the trains that came through so rarely were nil. We decided to risk it, however.

Mama ran along the train like a madwoman trying to persuade some conductor to take a child "for any money you want." The train only stopped for five minutes. A conductor in the same car in which our friends were traveling agreed. I didn't even have time to say good-bye to Mama or Sister. They thrust me and my things on the baggage shelf, on top of a mountain of dusty mattresses, and ordered me not to give a sign of life until called. I lay quiet as a mouse in the dust, snuggling up to a hot pipe and trembling with excitement. I lay there eight hours without sneezing or stirring. I had one little accident, but there was no way out—better to lie in dampness than be put off the train. They let me get down only after we left Krasnoyarsk, where the conductor who'd agreed to accompany me bought me a ticket from Krasnoyarsk to Moscow, and I was converted from stowaway into passenger.

Exactly six years had gone by since they had taken us over this very track in freight cars, not knowing where we were going or why. It was here I'd learned my first Russian word, *bweechkee.* And now I was traveling like a lady to the capital of our country, and on a grown-up's ticket, too. I felt clever, independent, determined, and proud. It's true I was small and not much to look at, but that wasn't important. I was full of hope.

*Act II*


# M O S C O W – K A U N A S


Uncle deliberately took a taxi from the station just to overwhelm an awkward country girl. Moscow stunned, dazed, and astounded me, but Uncle's room dealt me the crowning blow. I knew he worked in a ministry, but that two people could occupy so grand a room alone had never entered my head. It was twenty meters square, with big windows opening on the courtyard. There was a telephone on the desk. My aunt had a real dressing table with all sorts of jars on it. Uncle and Aunty slept in a handsome nickel-plated bed; I was given the couch. The dining table and chairs stood in the middle of the room. It's true there wasn't room to open the doors of the huge buffet all the way, but you could get things out of it without moving the table. There was a clothes cupboard in the room, too.

I liked my aunt very much. I did my utmost to make a good impression and remember all Mama's instructions: Don't make faces, don't interrupt the grown-ups, don't speak your opinion first, don't ask for anything.

The apartment wasn't very big; there were just five families sharing with Uncle, but not all of them lived as grandly. In one family, there were three children and the father was an invalid. They were almost as crowded as we were in Kansk or Dzerzhinsk.

I dreaded using the toilet. It seemed to me that if I didn't pull the chain just right, the water would run over the edge and flood. Whenever there was no one in the kitchen next door, I'd run in for a jug of water, which I felt was enough instead of that huge amount, most of which was completely wasted. But the neighbors soon complained to my aunt, who explained to me how everything was to be done. She taught me to wash in the mornings at the sink in the communal kitchen, where the lodgers came with their own soap dishes, tooth-brushes, tooth powder, and towels. I, as usual, used to barely sprinkle my face and hands with a little water for the sake of appearances, and then run, dripping, down the long corridor to our room, and grab anyone's towel. That was also taboo, but I'd never had a towel of my own before.

For weeks, I jumped with fear every time the telephone rang, and my first meal with my aunt and uncle destroyed my peace of mind for a long time after. From the first, my aunt asked me to set the table and explained how it was done. I found everything, but had no idea what it was for. She showed me. I thought it all very pretty, but quite unnecessary. Why should I have a napkin, for instance? Or why should each person have a spoon, a fork, and a knife besides? I knew how to use a spoon quite skillfully, though Aunty said it was not correct to shove the whole spoon in one's mouth, that one should eat from just the tip. I wondered what she'd say if she'd seen me in the village deliberately shoving a great wooden spoon in my mouth. And how she would have liked eating the way people eat in the village, all out of one wooden bowl and with only spoons for everything—cabbage soup, potatoes, and kasha. And Mama used to hit us with her spoon when we started fighting at the table.

Aunty showed me how to hold a fork. The knife I mastered only later. The whole dinner was nothing short of amazing, I'd never eaten like that since my childhood. There was even a compote.

Afterward, we took a walk to admire Moscow. Uncle bought me some ice cream at the Chisty Pond, saying playfully it was S on a stick (he meant shit on a stick). It wasn't S at all, as Uncle said, but sweet, tasty, and dazzling. How spoiled they were. Now I understood why my sister loved Moscow so, and I thought to myself, "Hah, they're not going to have a chance to think I might get in trouble with some boy, I won't make that mistake. I'm going to stay in Moscow."

But complications arose. You couldn't live in Moscow without a permit and to get one you had to have a very convincing reason. I had nothing of the kind. Uncle went to the militia and brought back application forms. As on all questionnaires, place of birth and social origin were the items Uncle feared because they could endanger his job. Of course, he didn't have a very responsible position, but it was still better not to have a niece with that kind of answers on her questionnaire.

School presented a problem too. There was a model school for girls in Shcherbakovsky Area, where we lived. You had to study in the area in which you had a permit to live, so once I had a permit for that area, I could study only in that school. However, the school didn't want to take me because my certificate of having completed seven grades and my conduct record (though I had *fours* for behavior) were both issued in Siberia, and that didn't ring the right note for that kind of school.

My aunt thought I wouldn't be able to keep up in that school anyway. I felt she was right; I really didn't know how to behave. I heard that from her, too, all day long. What became of all my resolutions? I'd talk myself into being reasonable and find myself having another philosophical argument with my aunt instead.

"Why can't you get used to hanging your things in the cupboard?"

"Because we didn't have cupboards. Everything lay on the bed or the stool at home, and we kept most of our clothes in a suitcase under the bed. How could I be used to using cupboards?"

"Dishes should be dried with a special towel after washing, I've already told you that."

"What for? I see why we wiped them at home—because we didn't rinse them, and we only heated water for very dirty dishes or when something burned or dried on them. But here, you wash them well in warm water and use as much again on rinsing. The dishes shine like mirrors and you want to dry them on top of that? It's a pity to use up a towel, you just have to wash it sooner."

Why do I eat cutlets with a spoon? Why don't I use a napkin instead of wiping my mouth with the palm of my hand? Why do I still refuse to flush the toilet? Why do I bang the door? Why do I always shout when I answer the telephone? What's this trick of sliding down the banister? My aunt spouted an uninterrupted stream of "whys" for which I always found what I felt were completely reasonable explanations.

Then a letter came from Mama. They gave it to me only that evening when Uncle came home from work. Opened. And on the envelope was written, perhaps as a joke, that it was for me *personally*, even underlined. While I read it, I kept wondering how to ask diplomatically who had dared open *my* letter.

"Did it come open?"

"No, I opened it," Aunty answered drily.

"Why?"

"To read it, of course."

"But it's addressed to me."

"Well, what of it? You don't think you're so grown-up you don't have to be supervised, do you?"

"No, I don't. But you don't think my relations with Mama need to be supervised, do you? I could hardly get pregnant through that kind of relation."

My aunt reddened, my uncle scowled. I felt frightened.

Soon after that, my cousin from Kaunas came to get me. I was a difficult child.


KAUNAS

Kaunas wasn't Moscow—no streetcars, no trolleybuses, no subway. But there was an elegant four-room apartment with a bath and no one to share it, and there was my kind, jolly aunt and my wonderful uncle—who, I later learned, wasn't my aunt's husband at all, but first the friend and later the husband of her daughter. Behind the kitchen they fixed me a separate room where they'd kept firewood until then. There was just space for a narrow couch, a tiny table, a stool, a bookshelf, and a little vase with flowers.

I was very happy. Everything went swimmingly. With no complications, I was accepted in the only Russian girls' school, in fifth grade, which corresponded to eighth grade in grammar school. I was well treated at home and at school, there was lots to eat, and everything was very good. The Lithuanian tongue was a little trouble at first. They all read, sang, and recited poetry aloud in class, while I didn't know the alphabet, but I learned fast. My aunt's maid, Yulya, helped me to do my homework in Lithuanian. She was half illiterate, it's true, but knew something just the same.

In 1947, a few months after my arrival, two events took place, currency reform and the end of rationing.

The reform made no sense. If you'd had ten rubles, now you had one. But for reasons I didn't understand, several people in Kaunas committed suicide because of this reform. On the other hand, I was able to appraise at once the end of rationing because it meant still more good things to eat in the house. Every day after the noon meal, I was sent to the Tulpa café for pastry. It was like sending a fox after chickens. On the way back, I licked, pinched, and squeezed all the filling I could out of the pastries without their falling apart. I assume my aunt and uncle guessed because the pastries looked pretty pitiful after I got through trimming them. To their eternal glory, my aunt and uncle never reproached me. And when reserves of bread, sugar, candy, and buns were found under my pillow, where I'd stored them because I knew anything could happen in life—then, too, no one reproved me. My aunt simply threw them out and quietly waited for me to get over my fear of hunger.

The school was close to our house and amusingly situated. Two sides looked out on the street; the other two on the cemetery. This struck the teachers as unfortunate, the students as delightful. It was in this cemetery that I had my first kiss.

We attended school in two shifts, girls in the morning, boys in the afternoon. There were few local Russians in the school, most of them children of officers in the border guard. Though there were lots of Russian soldiers in the city, they weren't allowed to bring their families. Whenever one of the girls in my class visited me in my little room behind the kitchen, the maid Yulya would rattle the dishes ostentatiously and sing badly in Lithuanian and Polish. Her hatred for the parents carried over to the children; she considered them all occupiers. When she helped me study Lithuanian, it usually led to this kind of conversation:

"Missy, why do you bother my head with talk of

the Soviets? Did I invite them here? No. Does anybody else want them here? No. You tell me the living's gotten better. For whom? For the occupiers and spoiled brats like the ones that come to visit you. I used to work in a beer parlor, but I wasn't impudent like those hussies. Maybe you think we were badly off? Not at all. Why, when Smetona was president . . ."

And then we'd have a long spiel about how well Yulya had lived under Smetona. She was no rich lady, no, far from it, she served beer and washed dishes in a beer parlor. But she had everything a body needed. If she wanted to, she could go visit her brother in Poland; if she wanted to, she could take a trip to Riga with some guy. And now? This was forbidden, that was forbidden, for this you could go to prison, for something else, worse yet—get sent to Siberia.

"Do you know what Siberia's like, missy? No? Then let me tell you it's a place no one ever comes back from. I don't need their stupid movies. I don't need to be told what's good for me. What I like is laughing and dancing, being able to go to the beer parlor at night and talk about anything a body having a jolly time thinks of. Nowadays everybody says, 'Keep your mouth shut.' And these hundreds of papers you have to fill out for someone and in Russian, yet. What for? Under Smetona, there weren't any papers, pay was higher, everything was cheaper, and everyone was content. There. And you tell me living's better now. Ah, missy, you're young and I feel sorry for you. You'll never have the thing that's most important—freedom."

I met *him* on the broad school stairway. For the first time, I looked deep into a man's eyes, held my breath, and was lost. His eyes were gray and very beautiful. It happened on my birthday. I'd been given a thick notebook, and I decided to start keeping a diary in honor of those eyes. I had just turned fourteen that day; the young man, Gleb, was fifteen. I later learned my eyes looked gray and beautiful to him, too. We became friends.

He lived in the dormitory for children of officers stationed in parts of Lithuania where there were no Russian schools. I envied the boarders because they breathed the same air he did.

We met almost every day, but only for a few minutes. I was kept on a tight rope—"home no later than eight." I knew I had to be there—otherwise, I'd have to sit on the stairway. But twice a week I went to do gymnastics in the Officers' Club, and those days, Gleb would accompany me home. When we met by chance on the school staircase, I blushed all the way to my feet, blinked watering eyes, muttered something idiotic, and walked past on unsteady legs, my heart pounding. I was in love forever.

His social origins were obviously better than mine. His father was the head of the NKVD in the town of Mariyampole, several hours' drive from Kaunas, but even that didn't disturb me. They had a private chauffeur, who came for Gleb on Saturdays—sometimes in a Willys, sometimes in his father's Mercedes, a war trophy. That pleased me, despite Yulya's opinion of occupiers. But I was scared to death he might ask me to tell him something about my own life and my father sometime. Just the thought made me turn red. "My God, how could I lie to the person I love most, the person I'm closest to on earth?" I learned to sniff out dangerous topics from afar. The moment a conversation touched on home, no matter whose, or parents, no matter whose, I skillfully changed the subject. To my credit, I succeeded. He never learned anything about me. I don't think he even knew I was Jewish. Given his social origins, he might have found that disagreeable. However, we separated. He fell ill, his parents took him to Mariyampole, and in two months he was so far behind in his studies that he decided to repeat the course the following year.

I was miserable. I used to stare at the stars at night for hours and picture our meeting again, despite everything. We take each other by the hand; I force myself not to be so painfully shy. Perhaps I've even gotten better-looking and rounded out a little by then. Perhaps I even tell him how much I like him, and perhaps (here, I'd always begin to tremble), perhaps, he kisses me on the cheek.

I kept my diary religiously. Every day my entry began with the words: "I love him. Forever."

My friends arranged a surprise for me, and I saw *him* again on New Year's. I hadn't told anyone besides my diary how miserable I was, but the girls in my class obviously guessed and invited him for New Year's Eve. However, I hadn't gotten any better-looking during those months, hadn't rounded out, and was shyer still in awareness of it. I sat glumly in a corner. I was burning with love, but he came to the conclusion I had grown indifferent to him—so he said when he took me home. I had orders to be home promptly at eleven, an hour before the New Year struck, but he kept hold of my hand. My breathing suspended, I trembled as if I had a fever. In silence, we walked home and stood there a while. I was half an hour late and had to sit on the stairs for ten minutes in punishment. Promptly at midnight I deluged my pillow with tears in honor of my ardent and unrequited love. There had been no kiss on the cheek.

Gleb's parents sent him to Vilnyus to study the following year. They were very much against Kaunas. In despair, I sometimes thought they might have learned the truth about me. I saw Gleb once with a very pretty girl. We greeted each other politely and parted. I gave no sign, of course, but I thought I'd faint with jealousy.

I wanted to die. The entries in my diary still began with the same short sentence, but it was tainted with bitterness.

But for that, everything would have been splendid. Things went well in school, I rattled on fluently in Lithuanian and was an honors student. I read heaps of interesting books. Sometimes my uncle took me to evening movies where they showed films captured in the war: *Doublecross, Indian Tomb, Spring Days,* and others. They didn't teach you a thing, you just sat and enjoyed yourself while people sang and danced. I also went to concerts in the Officers' Club. Uncle used to give me tickets and I was even allowed to take a friend with me.

In ninth grade I began getting letters from boys offering friendship and sometimes even declaring love, but they left me indifferent. Men didn't interest me. I soon even began feeling physically repelled by them.

My uncle had a good administrative post in the art field, but it seems one could go downhill in that field as well as any other. I was sent after pastry less and less often, fewer and fewer good things appeared on the table, and there was talk of having to get rid of my beloved Saint Bernard, Othello, who ate too much. My aunt and uncle often whispered together and fell silent when I appeared. They stopped frightening me with talk about how I should start studying music because, after all, it wasn't for nothing they had a beautiful Steinway piano with a bust of Beethoven on it.

Yulya grumbled in the kitchen that she was no magician able to make beef stroganoff out of bones, and there was no keeping a maid if things went bad. She stopped paying attention to me. All at once, I felt I was a superfluous mouth. I would gladly have spared my relatives expense on my account, but where was I to go? The idea of returning to Siberia terrorized me. I tried to keep out of everyone's sight, I never asked for anything, I tried to be useful; I wanted so badly to repay their kindness. But I didn't know how to do anything, I was no good at all. I wasn't even able to get up by myself and had to be woken up for school. For a while, my aunt woke me, but in the ninth grade, when I became mature, Uncle suddenly began waking me up instead. He had a strange way of doing it. He'd open the door very quietly, come into my room in pajamas, lift the covers, and lie down beside me on my narrow bed. He'd snuggle up to me, stroke me, kiss me. I froze in his arms like a hare in a wolf's mouth. He had slobberly lips. I'd grit my teeth in revulsion, but he'd urge me in a whisper to be affectionate with him. I felt wretched, but revulsion was stronger than duty, I couldn't be affectionate. I understood only much later how heroic he was to limit himself to that when he woke me.

I had very rigid ideas such as, "A maiden's honor is above all," and "It's better to die than kiss without love." Though I never connected our relations at these awakening scenes with love, at times I was overcome with shame and loathing. Several times, at what seemed to me critical moments, I'd leap out of bed with a cry and run, sobbing, into the kitchen. Uncle, red-faced and disheveled, would run after me, cover my mouth, and tell me not to say anything to anyone. It's strange he respected my "maiden's honor" because it seemed to me he "woke" me with my aunt's knowledge. First, he had to go through her room, and, second, as soon as he returned to his own room after the "awakening," she'd appear in the kitchen to get my breakfast. What held him back, I don't know, but I'll remember those scenes all my life. It came to an end very simply. One day I told my aunt that if Uncle came to wake me one more time, I'd jump out the window. She promised to straighten things out.

I soon discovered that my beloved diary, liberally sprinkled with bleeding hearts pierced with arrows, was being perused daily by my aunt. In the margins, I had drawn what I considered very accurate sketches of Gleb's magic profile with the black brows growing across the bridge of his nose and his gray eyes with long, turned-up eyelashes. Underneath, I'd write: "S plus G = LOVE." To think of things like that in outsiders' hands! My aunt got so used to this vile occupation that she sometimes forgot to remove her bookmarks. I was terribly upset at first and ready to lash out with angry accusations, but I remembered my bitter experience with my aunt in Moscow. There were no more aunts in reserve and Siberia was not tempting.

I tried hiding the diary. My aunt found it even in the food cupboard in the hall between my room and the kitchen. I hung it on a string behind the bookshelf; she found it. Not writing about my love for Gleb was impossible; hiding what I wrote was also impossible. Very well, I began to use my only friend, so dear to my heart, to tell inquisitive, dishonest people how disgusting it was to stick one's nasty nose into others' secrets. Comments on all sorts of unattractive domestic scenes also began to appear on the pages of my diary. My mockery was wasted; my aunt's curiosity got the upper hand. I even think that with her good-natured, cheerful disposition, she probably enjoyed this one-sided correspondence.

In ninth grade, I underwent a fundamental change. First of all, I rounded out, in some places significantly more than necessary, and that made me miserable, too. I had grown up. More important, I had somewhat revised my attitude. I became keen on community work. First I became editor of the school wall-newspaper, writing malicious satires with enthusiasm, drawing annihilating caricatures, and firing deafening blasts at boys for their lack of regard for state property (they sometimes carved initials—often mine—on the desks with penknives at night).

Then I was elected Komsomol secretary. I was very pleased about that, but for a very special reason. My being elected to such an important post meant my questionnaires weren't being checked out, which meant no one knew about Papa and Mama. I realized *this* was something to hide behind. Of course, the thought was rather at odds with pure Marxist-Leninist principles about the selfless, idealistic dedication of a Komsomolka, the Party's supporter and helper. But I knew I wouldn't last long in this world without my new philosophy.

Then began a series of meetings, debates, conferences, discussions, resolutions, studies, elaborations, reports, accounts, verifications—by and large, simply a matter of being present. Everything was worked out and approved by someone in advance, but we had to pretend we were taking part.

I acquired a bosom friend, Lyalya, who shared a desk with me. We used to write each other notes in class in which we said how lucky we were to have found each other. We exchanged impressions about our admirers and whispered together about love. We represented each other in these matters. My suitors turned to Lyalya for help, and hers turned to me. Whole poems were devoted to me, and I got lots of sonnets in the style of Petrarch, but they left me untouched. I was still in love with Gleb, though only Lyalya knew it. She, and my aunt.

Near the end of ninth grade, we were told that students who had all *fives* on their records could do independent study in the summer holidays and try their luck on the tenth-grade exams. If they passed, they would be skipped to the eleventh grade. I immediately took fire at the idea. I wanted very much to become independent. I persuaded Lyalya.

Matters at home were obviously going badly. My aunt
told me they had written my Moscow uncle, who'd agreed
to take me for the summer, and then—we'd see. Her
"Then we'll see" upset me greatly. "Then" I might have
to go back to Kansk. But what could I do? I consoled
myself by thinking I was a "philosopher" now, not a
green idealist just let out of Siberia. I had mastered the
knife and fork, and wouldn't react to having a letter
opened . . . I could handle anything.

My Moscow uncle and I met on the best of terms.
This time, we took a bus home from the Byelorussian
Station instead of a taxi. We had a serious talk, and I
tried to behave with discretion. It was a wonderful
summer. We walked around Moscow, went to the Sokol-
niki and the Gorki Park of Culture and Rest, went boating
on the Moscow River, heard a wonderful concert in the
hall of the Conservatory. That summer, I became fond
of music. But my tenth-grade textbooks, threatening and
untouched, cast a shadow over my life. I barely managed
to "run through" them, and what good is "running
through" in algebra, geometry, trigonometry, or
chemistry? I'd been at odds with mathematics from our
first encounter anyway.

I remember my earliest attempts to penetrate the secrets of algebra. I was still in the seventh grade. With
a note of weariness and contempt, my sister was explaining it, drawing me a kind of magic rite with symbols,
$A$s and $B$s, squared and cubed, sometimes with
parentheses, sometimes without. Then, without a
moment's hesitation, she casually dashed off some terribly ingenious answers in which the simple $A$s and $B$s
were doubled and tripled.

"Now do you understand?"

"No. Answer me in plain Russian: How much is $A$
plus $B$?"

"I just wrote it out for you."

"Answer me, give me a figure."

"But this is supposed to be an overall formula, not a specific problem. Understand?"

"No."

"Forget about figures. Imagine a mathematical law expressed in abstract symbols."

"I don't understand abstract symbols, give me the figures."

"Oh Lord, what can you do with such an idiot? Look, here's the formula. From this, it follows that—"

"What 'follows'? Why make such complications? And don't pretend you understand any of this, you're just putting on airs with your 'It's abstract' and 'It follows.' "

She threw me a weary, hopeless look and walked away.

When I returned to Kaunas with the family's consent, after my summer in Moscow, I passed the exams in literature, history, and geography with high marks. Obviously only out of regard for my achievements in those fields, I received a bare *three minus* in mathematics. I couldn't tell a cosine from a tangent. Lyalya passed the exams, too, and so did our mutual friend, Fanya. The three of us were promoted to eleventh grade.

My last year in Kaunas was filled with significant events. The most important was meeting Gleb again. We walked through our school cemetery, read each other verses, talked about life. I was madly in love with him, but he never knew it. It was drizzling. We sat on someone's grave with his jacket over our heads and my heart beating loudly. That evening, in the cemetery, he gave me my first kiss of love—pure, frugal, solitary, and brief. Many times later I sat with my head on someone's shoulder, not in the cemetery and not under a jacket, and exchanged kisses that were not so short and awkward, but I never again knew such a deep feeling of pure happiness.

My article about the work of our school Komsomol organization, whose secretary I still was, was printed in the young people's newspaper. I felt terribly embarrassed but unspeakably proud when I got my first few rubles of author's fees.

Because of my Komsomol duties, I often attended teachers' meetings at which general matters were discussed. At one stage, we were told the Komsomols should take the lead in school in seeing that proper emphasis was given to the universal struggle against the increasing numbers of rootless "cosmopolites." Dangers lurked in our textbooks. They sometimes failed to make it quite clear that every scientific discovery and invention had been made by a Soviet, or, if it happened to fall during the accursed time of the tsars, by a Russian, at least. I had already had experience in removing undesirables from textbooks—one finger in the inkwell, and out went the objectionable face. But it was 1949 now, no longer the difficult war years. Living standards had risen so much that we could afford to remove politically illiterate textbooks in their entirety. The vanguard of the Party, the Komsomols, were supposed to display particular vigilance at this task.

At that time, there were even worse people than the rootless cosmopolites in Lithuania, people who didn't just fail to acknowledge Russian or Soviet preeminence, but fought against it with weapons, too. They were caught, shot, exiled, and eradicated. Among the eradicated were a friend of my first cousin's, along with her mother and other members of the family. They lived next to us, but one night they just disappeared. I heard our bell ring, then heard running, whispering, and crying, but I stuck firmly to my private motto, "Don't crawl out until they make you." Our neighbors' son had disappeared from the house and hid in the woods with partisans who did not want Lithuania to be a Soviet republic. I didn't envy our neighbors; I felt very sorry for their beautiful daughter. It wasn't hard for me to imagine what awaited them in Siberia. That morning, it was whispered throughout the apartment building that during the night there had been a particularly widespread drive to eradicate all former, present, and potential enemies.

I felt I had acquired self-control; I decided to become a skeptic in addition. There was reason enough to do so. When I returned from my summer in Moscow, three of my favorite books had disappeared from my shelf: Chekhov, Tolstoi, and Gogol, all published by Wolf in thick blue bindings with oval relief portraits of the authors. All had obviously gone to the secondhand bookseller. Then a present from my aunt, a gold ring with a handsome stone, disappeared. Next, a big piece of real amber, Lyalya's birthday present to me. I took it all in silence, though I deeply regretted the loss of the books. It was only when I discovered my treasured stamp collection was missing that I timidly asked if it couldn't, perhaps, be found. Uncle, angry and embarrassed, said he had told me thousands of times already he would not let me keep that trash in his house, with all those stamps of all sizes with portraits of Hitler—it was disagreeable and dangerous. And since I hadn't obeyed him, he had burned them. "But why the whole album?" "So you'd be more obedient in the future." I was deeply hurt, but I no longer cried.

School gave me additional reasons for becoming a skeptic. We were taught astronomy and Latin by a bilious old gentleman we called Sir Slendzinsky, because he wore old-fashioned clothes, even used a monocle, and reminded us of the days before "comrade" replaced "sir." There weren't any Latin textbooks in those days, so Sir Slendzinsky wrote out excerpts from speeches by Cicero and other great Romans in notebooks for us in his elegant handwriting. We had to copy them five to ten times, depending on his mood. If my homework wasn't done, Sir Slendzinsky would say, "You naughty child, I'll have to go complain to your aunt today." That wasn't at all frightening. My aunt would serve him tea in the kitchen, give him bits of dried bread and sometimes even a scrap of soap to boot. Afterward, I wouldn't have to bother about Cicero and the other Romans for a month or more.

Sometimes Sir Slendzinsky would make up sentences for us to translate into Latin such as, "A spot has appeared on the sun, which means there'll be war," or "To be courageous, one must be honest." But someone didn't like Sir Slendzinsky's references to war and courage. First he was called before the regional Party committee, where he was threatened and accused of being apolitical. After that, we had other sentences to translate, like: "There are little flowers blooming in the fields, which means summer has begun." When he came to my aunt's for the ritual bit of soap, he said, "Do you think they need Latin? You can go to prison just as well without it." He didn't last out the school year—he disappeared. We weren't tested in Latin on the government exams, we were simply graded according to the previous term, and our geography teacher prepared us for the exams in astronomy.

When the time came for the government exams, I was scared to death about mathematics, though I'd gotten all *fives* throughout the year, thanks to Lyalya. Lyalya was terrific in math, and I used to write compositions for her in return. We did the same thing on the exams, too. I wrote two compositions on different themes and Lyalya solved all the math problems for me. The crib notes I sneaked in helped me through the orals in mathematics, so that I got *fives* in all eleven subjects. That entitled me to a gold medal, which meant I could enter a university without exams. I was dreaming of studying philology or, preferably, journalism, but I didn't tell anyone, even Lyalya, about it.

It turned out, however, that our school was only allowed one gold medal, which had to be given to a Russian, or at least a Lithuanian, as a representative of the aborigines, and in no case to a Jew. That's what the class master explained, a literature teacher who had been very nice to me. He then told me it had been impossible to lower my grade in mathematics to a *four* because it was, after all, such an exact science, so they had decided to lower my grade in composition. That's how the "friendship between peoples" licked the gold off my medal.

# L E N I N G R A D

I fell in love with Leningrad long before we met, back in Siberia, in my dreams. But I had never pictured myself there in reality, I'd merely thought up strange fantasies in which I played a leading role. Sometimes I was Nastenka of *The White Nights*, sometimes I was Liza in *Queen of Spades*, but most often, I was the fascinating Mystery Lady, borne by my imagination in a carriage with my coat of arms on the doors and a team of six horses all the way to Paris. My imagination always failed at Paris. As for Leningrad—there it was. I was standing in the square in front of the Moscow Station, alone, with the address of some people my uncle knew in my pocket. There had not even been time to let them know I was coming.

But, as always, I was lucky. The first person I asked how to get to Gesslerovsky Avenue took me by the arm, led me to the right streetcar, helped lift my suitcase up, and told the conductor to let me off at the right stop. The conductor was a good soul. He asked where I was from, where I was going, and "Oh'd" and "Ah'd" over a child of just seventeen traveling alone to a big city where she might be accosted at every step, where they could take the watch right off your wrist without your noticing, and if you had any money in your handbag, you'd better hold on to it tight every moment. He didn't forget about Gesslerovsky, he even told me how to get to the house. Uncle's friends happened to be at home, too, and though they weren't overcome with joy at seeing me, they agreed to let me leave my things and, if necessary, sleep there for a few days until I got into a student hostel.

I had come to study literature. Of all my previous enthusiasms—ballet, astronomy, driver training, and even aeronautics—literature alone had lasted.

My graduation certificate announced in large, glittering, silver letters: "This certificate, issued by virtue of paragraph 4 of the law ratified by the Soviet People's Commissar of the U.S.S.R., May 30, 1945, gives the possessor of gold and silver medals the right to enter a higher institution of learning in the U.S.S.R. without entrance examinations."

Amen.

All the same, they didn't want to take me without entrance exams. They didn't want to take me with them either. First the Russian and journalism departments fell through. I actually believed all places for medal winners were filled, though it seemed a little odd that the admissions committee told me this only after a hasty glance at my application instead of right away. I asked to be allowed to take exams with everyone else.

"What are you saying, girl? That's out of the question! Your country gives you the right to enter *without* exams, not *with* them. We're not allowed to change the law, you know. A medal is a medal."

They advised me to try my luck in other faculties of the University.

"But I want to study philology!"

"We've told you, the openings for medalists are filled. Don't bother us!"

I tried my luck in other faculties, tried it in other institutes. Everywhere, I encountered the same strange phenomenon: a smiling reception—"it's an honor for the institute to have medalists enter," a request to fill out forms, advice, promises about a hostel, and then, after a study of my application form, the faces of the directors of the admissions committee would be darkened by a slight cloud.

"You know, we'll have to check whether we haven't already taken our quota of medalists. As I remember it, we were more interested in gold medals. But don't lose heart, come back to find out tomorrow."

Or:

"Leave your papers, take your certificate. We'll let you know the decision of the admissions committee."

And they would advise me to visit other institutes. As for theirs, best just give them a call.

I visited, called, waited for decisions. Openings for medalists were closed everywhere.

Then I called one of the then least popular technical institutes and asked, "Have you filled all your openings for medalists?"

"No. Why do you ask?"

"I want to enter your institute."

"What's it all about, if you please?"

"I'm Jewish."

The silence made my heart start pounding, but then the voice said, "What difference does that make? Come over. You can come right now, if you hurry."

I had to pick my department out of the *Guide for Entering Students* because I was totally unfamiliar with technical subjects. They enrolled me, registered me for a grant, and arranged for a hostel right then and there. I was in ecstasy. I'd had reason to be desperate. My uncle's friends, who had just one room, obviously didn't appreciate my presence. I didn't even take tea in the mornings, just darted out the door unwashed and uncombed, but they had asked me to leave all the same. Once again, my philosophy and skepticism helped me: "If Jews are excluded or so severely restricted in the humanities, there's no point in trying to butt in. Even if they took me, what hope would I have of becoming a respected journalist or writer if they put so many obstacles in my path from the start? And for what reason? Only because of my nationality. Very well, then. Better for me to be an honest, average engineer than a lowly journalist or writer."

The only thing that bothered me was that I hated mathematics. But I was determined to get a higher education one way or another, at any price, even if it meant mastering all the technical sciences I hated.

My hostel was on the corner of Sredny Prospect and one of the numbered streets on Vassilievsky Island. A turnover was just under way, and secondary-school graduates were housed all together on one of the five floors. I had permission to stay there for the three weeks until school opened on the first of September. I had very little money, no place else to go, and decided to spend the whole time in Leningrad.

The city bewitched me. Sometimes I felt I knew it all, but all I knew were the names of the streets and squares. I walked to save money and ate twice a day at dairy counters, but everything tasted good there, and you see more on foot. I picked out famous sites to rest in such as the Summer Garden, the Fortress of Peter and Paul, or the point of Vassilievsky Island. There I'd daydream about beautiful women, jealous husbands, hussar admirers, perfumed love letters, and fast horses. And, of course, duels—sometimes on the ice of the Neva, sometimes by the Black River. Not surprisingly, I played more than a minor role.

The Hermitage dazzled me with its marble and gold,

made my head ache from looking at pictures. I preferred the Russian Museum, where the pictures were ones I'd known in school. In the Mikhailovsky Garden, I dreamed of murders.

Nowhere were you allowed to walk, sit, or lie on the grass; signs warned you about it at every step. But if you walked through the Field of Mars and crossed the Kirov Bridge, you could stretch out on a tiny strip of so-called beach beneath the Fortress of Peter and Paul. I had no bathing suit and would have been embarrassed to undress if I had had one, but my weary feet were quickly refreshed in the water.

There, too, I daydreamed, but my fantasies, which started with the Decembrist heroes and their loving and faithful wives, followed them all the way to Siberia (though they traveled in their own carriages, or, at worst, by post chaise), and stubbornly led me on to Mama and my sister, whom I hadn't seen in three years now and missed very much, and to my father, who might now be locked up in some stronghold like the architectural marvel before me, the Fortress of Peter and Paul. Sadness stole over me.

On the point of Vassilievsky Island, I fancied capricious beauties in crinolines daring playful glances over elegant fans at handsome young men on prancing horses.

It was very near here that the legendary cruiser *Aurora*'s guns had heralded the start of the revolution. Comrade Kirov himself had walked in this very spot before being felled by an evil hand quite close by, in the Palace Square. Lights shone from the countless windows of the Winter Palace that revolutionary Petrograd once stormed—but none of this entered my head, though I'd read about it and we'd had to memorize it, and there were films about it and even pictures of it in museums. Instead of Comrade Kirov's footsteps, I heard the hoofbeats of the Bronze Horseman and the roar of flooding waters; instead of the *Aurora*'s guns, I heard the aria from the *Queen of Spades* and, somewhere near the Palace Square, Nastenka of *The White Nights* hurried home along the Moika Canal.

The first semester went by as in a dream. I woke up when I failed to get a good enough grade on the very first exam, on the technology of metals, and lost my scholarship. My new record book was embellished with a *three*, which I received only because kindly Professor Kotov had stretched a point and sinned against his favorite subject. I railed at myself, despised myself, but that didn't get me a scholarship. And I had to live—I had to get a diploma in something, no matter what. I simply hadn't realized that school was to be taken seriously. I'd felt I'd found freedom at last, with nobody to make me sit on the stairs for being half an hour late. I was enjoying myself—and there was plenty to enjoy.

After the brief, unpleasant business of washing each morning in the general washroom, where you had to line up for the faucet, the days were a succession of delights. Clusters of students without tickets hung from the streetcars, hiding from the conductor. Then the whole jolly crowd poured on foot around the corner to Nevsky Prospect, past the Admiralty Building, took a short run through a back street, and flooded through the revolving doors of the Institute. Inside, there were lectures you didn't have to listen to at all, laboratory sessions you could slip through with somebody's help, and long jolly lines at the buffet for tea and in the dining room for cabbage soup and cutlets. Going home was the best part, walking across the Palace Bridge, down University Quay, past the granite sphinxes brought back to the capital city of Saint Petersburg in 1832 from ancient Egypt.

I rarely walked home alone; someone always appeared at my side as if by chance. Walking with George was

the nicest; the girls we passed would always look at him,
which made me swell with pride. He sang and told stories
marvelously. For a long time, I didn't dare ask him to
talk about his past for fear he might suddenly think I
envied him or that I felt something lacking here. George
came from Albania, though he was born in Sicily. His
mother was Italian. It was doubtless from her he inherited
his magnificent, warm voice.

"Tell me about Italy. Please. Tell me anything you
want, it fascinates me."

The stories and gentle Italian songs turned my head.
George noticed my emotion and laughed. "You have a
warm sea in the south here, too, blue, with beaches.
And hot sun and palm trees."

"But I'd like to see Italy once."

"I would, too."

"You—you can!"

"No. We can't either, I'm a Party member."

"So?"

"Don't be a child. We can't any more than you can."

"But you were born in Sicily, of course you can go
home!"

"Now we're on the subject, tell me, where were you
born?"

I froze with fear.

"Why do you want to know?"

"Why did you turn pale?"

"I'm not pale. Why did you ask?"

"Some days ago, I was called in to our national association and asked about you. I told everything I knew, but
I didn't know where you were born."

"But why? Why are they asking you about me?"

"Oh, that's simple. We foreigners aren't supposed
to become friendly with Soviet girls. We're warned about
that from the start. They'd seen me with you several
times, so they became interested. I said there was

absolutely nothing between us—simply acquaintances, you know, and told them what I knew."

"That should satisfy them. Then, are we never to see each other again? All we did was walk down the street and talk. What's wrong with that?"

"Nothing."

"And supposing a foreigner falls in love with a Soviet girl, then what?"

"They'd send him home. Or rather, before that, they'd talk to him as they did to me, warn him, explain marriage is forbidden, and then maybe things would straighten out."

"Did you know about that when you came here?"

"Yes."

"And do other foreigners know it?"

"Of course."

"Then what about Laslo and Laura? They even have a baby."

"Oh, that's a real tragedy. Don't I know! I was sharing a room with Laslo at the time. And that they were finally able to get married despite the difficulties doesn't mean a thing. They were told at the registry office that Laura still wouldn't be allowed to go to Hungary, though if Laslo wanted to, he could stay here."

"And then what?"

"I don't know. But I think he'll go."

"And leave her here with the baby!"

"Why does that bother you so?"

"Because I heard the girls in our room saying Laura wanted to kill herself when she found out they were going to have a child and couldn't get married."

"Laslo went through a lot, too. But I think this will all change."

Perhaps George was right in thinking this would change. But I was very much afraid of interest in my particulars on the part of any institution, and as for foreigners—no, I didn't need handsome men, I didn't need Italy, I could get along without songs. Something wonderful and unreal left with George. It was a pity.

Next, a Bulgarian was bold enough to start courting me persistently. He was fifteen years older than I, acted patronizing, brought candy, invited me to the operetta and the circus, and loved telling about his imprisonment, his activities in the underground, and, in general, how much he had done for his native land since he joined the Party. But this deserving Party member was summoned to his national association, too.

There were particularly large numbers of Chinese studying in Leningrad, but they never glanced at a Soviet girl, never came to the dances organized in corridors or on stair landings, talked to no one, and studied in special groups. They all dressed alike in dark-blue "Mao Tse-tungs." You often saw them picking their way along the wall in the hostels to the water boiler and back, almost stealthily, with the invariable teapot in hand. And at any hour of the night, you could see a shaven head and a "Mao Tse-tung" bent over books or diagrams in the "cram room."

My Kaunas friend, Lyalya, was studying in Leningrad, too. We saw each other almost every Saturday and were as close as ever, telling each other our most intimate secrets. We had friends in almost every institute, and it was a rare Saturday we didn't go to a dance somewhere. Sometimes it was at the Polytechnic, sometimes at the University, but most often in Lyalya's hostel or mine. We even went to the Artillery Institute and the Dzerzhinsk Naval Engineers Institute for parties. We began to expose ourselves to the arts together, too. We went to the Mariinka Theater for the first time to see

*Eugene Onegin.* At first we choked, laughing at the sight of the fat Tatyana, but little by little, we became captivated.

One has to know how to use freedom. I understood that too late, after getting a low grade on the very first exam. No scholarship was granted for a grade of *three*, and I saw no solution. I certainly didn't want to go back to Siberia, but I had nothing to live on. However, fate clearly had a hand in preventing Mama from getting rid of me when I was an embryo. Once again, fate stepped in, and my Moscow uncle rescued me. He had just signed a contract for three years in Sakhalin. On learning of my situation, he arranged to send me part of the money from the room in Moscow, which he had rented. This portion was even a bit more than my scholarship had been, about two hundred and ninety rubles, or thirty dollars per month.

I hadn't been living in the greatest luxury on my scholarship. I'd never worn silk stockings in my life, was totally ignorant of cosmetics, and only dreamed of getting rich enough one day to have a manicure and see a restaurant with my own eyes. I licked my lips when I saw the endless lines in the store on Sredny Prospect where they sold synthetic fabrics. After I'd paid the dormitory fee and my Komsomol and *Profsoyuz* (professional union) dues, there was rarely enough left to last until the next installment of my scholarship without going into debt. More often than not, toward the end of the month, there wasn't even enough for meatless cabbage soup in the student dining room. But we managed. Almost all the girls in our room were without a cent at the end of the month. Then we'd organize a collective meal in our room, buy potatoes, a sausage we called Marusya's poison, a lot of bread—fortunately there was always plenty of boiling water—and we'd have a feast.

I swore fearful oaths that I'd start studying, become serious, and stop running around to dances. I heaped shame on myself and others did the same. My case was introduced in the general Komsomol meeting as an example of how people don't know how to use freedom. Here I'd come to the Institute with a medal and gotten a *three* on the very first exam. If someone had told me then that I'd fail two subjects in the spring, I frankly wouldn't have believed it.

Mother wrote me cheerful letters, never complaining of anything. She advised me to study, to try to get a scholarship, to do everything I could so as not to depend on my uncle, "for anything can happen to a person."

In one of her letters, Mama mentioned a good friend of ours, an engineer, who: "Remember? Often came to visit us when we were still living with Aprokysa. Always hungry, unshaven, sometimes half incoherent? I used to scold you when you made fun of him. He was forever asking if there wasn't a crust of bread left from dinner. We were just thinking of the time he rushed over and tore a pot with some burned food in it out of my hands saying burned food was good for you. Remember?"

Mama wrote he had returned to his family in Leningrad, that he had a wonderful wife (who had gone to get him because he was too weak to make such a long journey alone), and that it would be nice if I visited them. They would be very glad to see me. "It's good to know there are good people around who'll stand by you in trouble." She enclosed a brief note to her friends.

They lived on Sadovaya Street. Judging by the fairly small number of bells at the outside door, the apartment was not particularly overcrowded. When our friend's wife opened the door for me, right there in the entrance, I introduced myself and congratulated her on her husband's safe return. What a hornet's nest I stirred up! Pale with fury, she grabbed me, covered my mouth, and dragged me into the room.

"You should be ashamed of yourself!" she whispered. "How can you pop up on people like that? Since when have well-brought-up people chatted in the entrance hall? They aren't deaf around here, they can all hear, it's no desert—and you shouting!"

"I'm sorry, I didn't realize I was talking so loud."

"We live in constant fear, we do everything we can so nobody will know, so the neighbors and people in general will forget what happened to us, we've gone through so much all our lives, and along comes this wretched girl, shouting as if to spite us."

"I wouldn't have come, it's Mama's thinking you'd be pleased. I'm sorry, I'd better leave."

"That surprises me even more. Your mother struck me as very intelligent, and my husband thought well of her. How could she fail to understand you shouldn't remind people of old terrors when life hangs by a hair?"

She was obviously genuinely terrified. She trembled and gasped, but I still didn't quite understand what harm I'd done.

"What are you staring like that for? All right, all right, I'm sorry, I shouldn't have greeted you like that, but you ought to be able to understand that we're trying to hide our past from the other people in the apartment. We had such trouble changing rooms. Our old neighbors made life unbearable when my husband was sentenced. Lord, what they didn't do, it's awful just remembering, and we couldn't complain, we'd have been sent to Siberia ourselves. No one in this apartment knows anything, and then you waltz in, shouting about a happy return from Siberia. Where's your head? How could you? Forgive me, I'm yelling at you again, but please, don't ever do that. I don't want to offend you and your mother, but you'd better not do it again. You're a big girl, you

ought to be able to understand. Just imagine what those
fifteen years my husband was in prison were like for
me and my daughter and you won't be angry if I ask
you not to visit us again. Right, dear?"

"Of course."

I wasn't offended. On the contrary, I was terribly
ashamed of having alienated good people through my
own stupidity. And they really were good people. After
I'd apologized, promised, and so on, they said if I ever
wanted to go to the movies with their Zhenichka, I should
just telephone and they'd buy me a ticket. We could
meet near the movie house.

I wrote Mama I didn't have time then to visit our
friends, but would do so without fail at some future date.

After that, when my uncle wrote from Sakhalin that
I should get to know his wife's relatives, I was prepared
for all sorts of surprises, and must confess I went with
a heavy heart. But it turned out well. They received me
cordially, fed me very well, asked about the Institute
and the dormitory, nodded approvingly when I said there
were six girls in my room, all of them wonderful, and
laughed at the way we pooled our resources. Papa,
Mama, and my sister were never mentioned. I was in
constant fear of saying something out of line, and I noticed
they exchanged glances from time to time, so I was glad
when dinner was over. They were, too, apparently. We
parted very amiably; they invited me to come anytime
I didn't have money for dinner, but I never went back.

It was only several years later, after my arrest,
imprisonment, and return to Siberia, that I understood
they had reasons and very pressing ones not to ask about
people who had been arrested when their own lives hung
by a hair. At the time, the head of the family had been
repacking his bundle of dry bread, underwear, and a
toothbrush every half year for fourteen years, in anticipa-
tion of arrest.

But I was only slightly offended at that time. At

seventeen, one doesn't want to think badly of life. Everything seemed wonderful, and I pushed these trifles out of my mind easily with the conclusion I didn't need anyone anyway.

At one of the dances in the dormitory, Shura, one of my roommates, whispered in my ear: "Don't look now, look later. In the corner across the room is a fellow who's watching you. He's the biggest swine ever. If he asks you to dance now, you're as good as lost, he's not easily gotten rid of. He'll ruin you. He's ruined lots of girls. I could tell you things about him that would make your hair stand on end."

"What's his name?"

"Oleg."

"A beautiful name. And he himself is quite—"

"Exactly what I was saying," Shura hissed angrily. "That's how he ruins us girls."

"But Shurochka, he hasn't done anything to me yet! Can't I even look at him?"

"No. And he'll do it. He does it to everyone. You're as big a fool as all the rest. You're already hooked with your *quite* . . . "

Oleg was walking slowly across the empty dance floor in our direction. The moment the gramophone crackled before the start of the next record, Shura grabbed me and started dancing. I hated dancing with girls, though it was the accepted thing then because the girls outnumbered the men by more than three to one. Somehow I always managed to get a male partner, however. I let Shura know how I felt by acting stiff.

"Shurochka, why be so mean?" a very pleasant voice said in our ears, but Shura hugged me tighter. "I don't eat people."

Shura whispered in my ear, "Leave, leave right now before the music's over. He won't leave you alone. If you don't go, you'll dance the next dance with him and then everything will be lost."

"But I like him."

Shura dropped me in the middle of the dance floor. I danced with Oleg until the end of the evening. He danced divinely, dressed better than the others, and behaved irreproachably. If he was a swine, it didn't concern me. He asked how I liked Leningrad, where I came from, what department I was in, and if my studies were going well. About himself, he said he was in his fifth year, would graduate from the Institute in a year, was already working half days, and had picked the subject of his thesis. After defending his thesis, he'd probably stay to work in Leningrad.

His voice was quiet, soft, and very cheerful. He listened attentively, without interrupting. We parted before the last dance. He didn't even arrange to meet again.

A week later, on Saturday, I pressed my only dress with great care and went to the dance with a fluttering heart. Oleg was there, but he danced alternately with two girls I didn't know—not students, just friends of his, apparently. He barely glanced at me. Shura, who hadn't spoken to me all week, sniffed smugly and threw me a withering look. "See?" Shortly before the evening was over, Oleg left with those two disgusting girls.

I was furious. The following Saturday, I went to a dance in Lyalya's dormitory. Oleg wasn't around at all for several Saturdays in a row and I would have forgotten all about him if it hadn't been for Shurochka. Every time she got a chance, she'd give me new details about his "stormy love life," which only fanned my curiosity.

When Oleg finally asked me to dance again, I suddenly started trembling in his arms, fawning on him, stuttering, talking nonsense, and generally behaving like an idiot. He noticed it, of course, but gave no sign. That made me angry, too, but I kept on trembling.

I liked Oleg very much.

One day the house porter came to tell me to go to the radio station that was in the same building. I froze. They couldn't be summoning me for anything good.

There I found Oleg. He officially informed me he'd like to test my voice. He was looking for a woman announcer, you see, and it seemed to him I had a pleasant voice and good diction. As you gather, he was the director of the radio station. The test was favorable, I displayed my diction successfully, and was taken on as alternate announcer.

We met daily, usually at the radio station. We took walks, went to the movies. I always found him interesting. I guess I fell in love. I used to reflect with shame what a wicked, immoral creature I was—I'd thought I'd be true to Gleb all my life. But Gleb was far away and Oleg was here. His behavior was irreproachable. I understood now why Shurochka had been so spiteful; it was simply that Oleg had failed to fulfill his ladies' hopes. They absolutely had to get themselves a husband; otherwise they'd be sent to the backwoods when the government assignments were made. Even if you got assigned to the sticks anyway, it was better to be two. Oleg, furthermore, had some chance of staying in Leningrad. No girl could resist that, while I could spit on it—I was only in my first year, and didn't have to think about where the government might send me yet.

My roommates soon got used to my coming home late—or, rather, early in the morning. I had to throw water on my face to wake myself up in the mornings. The days dragged on interminably, but toward evening—where did my energy spring from?—I'd fly to the radio station on wings to give a news broadcast.

The summer term approached. My work was in a sorry state. Differential (and later, integral) calculus and the Fourier series remained as mysterious and hateful as before. One of my classmates brought me written summaries of descriptive geometry, another one drew the exercises for me. I repaid them with reports in various styles of handwriting on the origins of Marxism-Leninism, and by masterful prompting at colloquiums. I had occasion to read and reread the works of Comrades Lenin and Stalin.

Our group was a mixed one—a few girls, age eighteen to nineteen, and the rest boys, much older, most of whom had been at the front. They were the ones who ran the show. For example, when we used to prepare for a colloquium on Marxism-Leninism, one of the "seniors" would take a part of the assigned topic and another would prepare the other part. The rest of the group wouldn't prepare anything that day. "Madame"—as we nicknamed Gurvich, our really nasty teacher of Marxism —would appear in the lecture room. With firm tread, she'd cross to the table, take roll call, and prepare to choose a victim. At that point, the boy with the first half of the topic would raise his hand.

"Nina Abramovna! I read Comrade Lenin very attentively in preparing for today's topic, but I don't think I quite understood the question he raised. Couldn't you explain it?"

"What do you mean? You didn't quite understand Comrade Lenin? Do you realize that aside from Comrade Stalin, no one has been able to present his thoughts as clearly and precisely as Comrade Lenin? You answer the question and together we'll clarify."

That was all we needed.

Then the voice of the second half of the topic would speak in the same spirit, and the bell would ring.

Blunders occurred, too, however.

"Madame" arrives. Someone cautiously introduces the topic:

"Just before you came, we were having a big discussion about the nationality question. And a disagreement arose. I completely agree with Comrade Lenin, while Zelentsov, here, considers Comrade Stalin more correct on that question. Please explain to us who's right and who's not, Nina Abramovna—it happens to coincide with the topic of our colloquium today."

During this introduction, Nina Abramovna stares fiercely at the speaker and no less fiercely at the silent group around. Taking a deep breath, she explodes.

"Never, you hear? Never has any disagreement, even the slightest, arisen between the two geniuses. You are therefore both wrong, and I am very earnestly concerned about this. In your place, Comrade Finkelstein, and also in yours, Comrade Zelentsov, I would guard against exhibiting my profound political illiteracy so lightheartedly. Furthermore, if I'm not mistaken, you are both members of the Party—the Lenin-Stalin Party, and you ought to know there's no discord in it. Stay after the session, both of you, I'll talk to you then. And now, we'll take up the nationality question."

Some unexpected grades of *two* would appear on that day's record.

I did well in only one subject, German language. We were required to be able to read and translate technical texts with the aid of a dictionary. Because my parents used to speak German together, I could translate easily without a dictionary, but was very afraid of being suspected of knowing such a dangerous subject as a foreign language too well. I used to mangle the pronunciation when reading aloud and I pretended to use a dictionary when translating, but I was still afraid someone might become interested in where and why I'd learned a foreign language. On the other hand, I was happy to help my comrades with translations, in return for which they did homework for me in various technical subjects.

I didn't pass my exams at the end of the spring term; I failed physics and mathematics. The reexaminations were in the fall, which pretty well spoiled the summer. Oleg had just passed his state exams with all *fives*. I was very ashamed. I was sorry to cause Mama grief and found it very awkward to write my uncle in Sakhalin, on whom my fate depended. The worst was that I knew perfectly well if I'd just paid a little more attention to mathematics and physics, I would have been able to pass; others were passing their exams somehow, you see, and I couldn't be dumber than they. It didn't lighten my heavy conscience a bit to tell myself the others had chosen to study here of their own free will, unlike me.

My relatives in Lithuania invited me for the summer. While I was there, I got a detailed letter from Mama in which I finally learned something about Father. Mama hadn't written about him, she hadn't even mentioned him in her letters to me in Leningrad for fear of spoiling my "clean" personal record, which said Papa had "died on the workers' front." He was in his tenth year in prison and was still granted no visits, but from time to time Mama got together a package for him of dried bread, tea, perhaps even a little jar of butter, and some honey. He wrote cheerful letters, never complained about anything, always asked about me, and wished me good health and prudence. Mama also wished me prudence. It was so important for me to remember at all times how cautious one had to be.

I always remembered I had to be careful. In my happiest moments, I remembered it. I was always on guard. The minute a forbidden topic was lightly touched upon, I'd sidestep with the dexterity of a juggler. My greatest triumph was that Oleg didn't know a thing about me, though he often asked stupid questions, which made me very angry. We almost quarreled once when Oleg suddenly, for no reason, became interested in my knowledge of German. I had just helped him translate something he needed for his work. He went so far as to blurt out, "It seems to me there's something not quite right about your family." Oh Lord, what an act I put on! I would rather have broken off with Oleg than think he suspected something.

My sister had left the mathematics department at the University of Tomsk to transfer to the Krasnoyarsk Medical Institute for some reason. She always visited Mama in Kansk in the summer. I longed to visit home, too, but it wasn't to be thought about—I had no money for the journey; and besides, it was dangerous.

Professor Metter was pleasantly surprised when I got a *five* in physics that fall.

"Then what happened to you last spring when I gave you a *two?*"

"It was spring, probably."

"What?"

"Well, you know, there's so many things going on in spring."

"Did you attend my lectures?"

"Of course! They always check up on us, it's impossible to skip. But before the reexamination, I didn't understand physics at all, or mathematics either. It was just this summer I suddenly felt it was within my grasp. But then, all technical subjects come hard for me."

"Then why did you choose the Technical Institute?"

"Oh, because—I just wanted to."

The professor looked at me a little more closely, opened my record book once more, leafed through it, compressed his lips. He understood. He wished me success in my studies. With difficulty, I got a *three* in mathematics. I was glad Oleg wasn't there. He would naturally have accused me of being stupid, but he had gone to his mother's for the summer. Graduate students returned from summer vacation a month later than we did.

My uncle continued to send me my monthly "stupidity grant." I promised myself to be serious, to study hard from the start, but it was very difficult. Something always interfered. This time it was a freshman. He danced with style, sang, got to know everyone quickly, soon fell into the habit of visiting us in our room, and was always delighting my roommates with his generous gifts—sometimes apples, sometimes plums, and always special ones, ripe and large. Things were very jolly when he was around. He was Greek, and his mother lived somewhere near Odessa. He himself was an actor in some provincial theater near Odessa and he spouted theater gossip. When I asked him about his father once, his yellowish eyes blinked just slightly longer than usual.

"I have no father."

"Did he die at the front?"

"No."

"On the workers' front?"

"Yes, how did you know?"

I made something up. But he looked around somewhat suspiciously and fearfully, and left earlier than usual. Something was not quite right about him, too. Such a jolly fellow, always making jokes, and suddenly so frightened—so he had a little wormhole, too. I wasn't really surprised. There were many exiled Greeks in Siberia, and I had the feeling they were exiled solely because of their nationality, like the Volga Germans. I felt sorry for our ham, as we called him among ourselves.

He jokingly swore eternal love to me and one day invited me to an operetta that had been very successful. It was about the great construction program. A hideous contraption representing a steamboat moved across the stage, going down the Volga to the great construction. "He" and "she" were on it. "He" was a builder of locks;

"she," an architect. "He" was on fire with the idea of the great construction; "she" would rather have lived in Moscow. In the evenings, leaning over the railing of the sputtering steamboat, they held hands while singing clumsy ditties about the good life in shrill, oily voices, while the intrepid captain, the sailors, and the workers who were also bound for the great construction diligently sang and danced in accompaniment. They all cooperated to protect the lady architect from the insidious intrigues of her former suitor, a prominent engineer and a scoundrel, who was trying to tempt her from the true path and persuade her to return to him in Moscow.

I was bored. In the first intermission, my companion, struck by the magnificence of the staging, the scenery, the felicitous lighting, the voices, and the excellent direction of certain scenes, overlooked my plaintive pleas to go home. He whispered some scandal about the actress and told a number of theatrical anecdotes. In the second intermission, I ran off. He stopped speaking to me. It was only when Oleg came back from vacation that I suddenly got a package of huge apples from the south with a note that Oleg was the first to read. Blushing as much with pleasure as embarrassment, I bit into an apple while offering one to Oleg. He pushed my hand away and asked me to spare him the disgusting presents of such upstarts, and added he would have nothing against my sparing him my own presence, too. I didn't leave. Then he spoke his anger:

"People like you can't be left alone for a minute, and I'm not ready to keep watch over you all my life. I have my own work to do. I can just imagine what you've been doing all summer. And I don't want to hear about it. Since everyone here knows you and I are friends, you might have behaved better if only out of regard for me, and in any case, not do the devil knows what with every fool that comes along. I'd barely gotten in the dormitory door when they started telling me about your antics. I probably wouldn't have said anything to you if this bum hadn't made such a point of making your relationship plain."

"We had no relationship. I've never had any relationship of any kind."

"Oh, I've been wanting to tell you for a long time how fed up I am with your prudishness, which seems to be confined to me for some reason."

I should have left, but didn't know how to. Oleg was probably right about my prudishness. I myself had decided long ago that virginity shouldn't be treated like a new toy, but he was wrong about its being confined to him. I felt pained and awkward. Slowly the idea dawned that jealousy is a sign of love. Meaning that Oleg loved me, though he had never said so. But why did it all sound so unattractive and even somewhat frightening?

We didn't meet for several days. Then the house porter brought a note saying: "You must fulfill your duties as announcer until a replacement is found." We made up. Oleg was very apologetic. He explained he had been infuriated by the sight of those big, beautiful apples, and, still more, by my self-satisfied expression. And then, they'd been brought on purpose when we were together. He hadn't really believed I'd behaved badly, and he'd wanted to say long ago that he loved me and wanted me to marry him.

I shed a tear of happiness. My first declaration of love, my first proposal. I murmured something very romantic, we embraced and kissed. It was very nice and not at all prudish. There was only that tiny hole that made itself felt all the time as if a worm were gnawing at my happiness—no marriage, ever. Forget that. If you love him, you don't want to spoil his life; his whole career would be finished.

Oleg was very tender, as if he sensed something. "What are you thinking about? Why are you crying? Do you want to tell me something? Tell me, don't be afraid, it won't change anything, it will only make things easier."

"What do you mean, dear? I'm simply very happy, you know everything about me. Everything entirely, now."

I began coming back to my room in the mornings.

That year, too, there were six of us in the room, but there was a difference of only two courses between us, not four, as in the previous year. Shurochka and the other girls had graduated that year, like Oleg.

We got along well, though we were a motley crew. My roommates were very serious about their studies. Discussions and quarrels often broke out in the room about highly technical questions, diagrams were drawn, calculations produced. I was usually silent with wonder and a little envious of their love for their field. However, partly because of their enthusiasm, partly because of Oleg's salubrious influence, I set myself to mastering the detested technical sciences and got good grades in the winter session with no *threes*. My greatest satisfaction was being able to write my uncle that I could now most gratefully refuse his lifesaving "stupidity grant."

My roommates became used to my relations with Oleg, who was a guest of honor in our room. Through all five years, he had had the highest grant for excellence in studies, he was often cited as an example at meetings, and my serious roommates were very impressed, the more so because he would explain so enthusiastically whenever they asked him technical questions. I felt proud.

We all had a hard time getting by. We gave practically no thought to clothes, though no one had more than two or three nondescript dresses, one coat, one pair of shoes, and rubber boots. The girls often exchanged dresses, but no one could wear mine because they were too tight. We economized like mad, but rarely managed to stretch our grants far enough, though we saved all we could, even stealing rides to and from the Institute without tickets. We tried cooking at home because it came out cheaper. All the soups—meatless cabbage soup, pea soup, potato soup, or barley soup—were seasoned with onions fried in lard. Almost everyone got lard from home.

The stores were full of produce: butter, milk, all kinds of milk products, sausages, canned goods. Bread and buns were plentiful. There were even all sorts of caviar and salmon for sale. Two kinds of canned crabmeat gathered dust on the shelves. Hardly anyone ever bought crab because people weren't used to such delicacies and it was more expensive than other canned goods. In just a few years, however, crab, salmon, and caviar simply disappeared from the stores along with many other things.

I never cooked at home for myself. Mornings and evenings, I'd have a bottle of chocolate milk with a roll. At midday, I had dinner in the student dining room at the Institute. I economized fiercely; I had a pressing reason for it. That summer, my relatives had given me a length of material for a coat, and I was burning to have my first real coat made in the latest style—very long, full, with what was then known as a "rippling back," a flared effect that was considered somewhat daring in those days. But, in addition to the material, I needed a lining, lapels of some sort, horsehair stiffening, buttons, and a collar. None of this was to be found on the open market. I got all the trimmings through friends, and the collar—dyed black rabbit—my relatives in Lithuania sent me as an additional gift after I wrote that for lack of a collar, I was still wearing my old coat, made over from one of my aunt's.

In the stores you could buy terribly expensive chiffon,

crepe de chine, dazzling satin crepe, and stunning panne velvet, which only Party members' and officers' wives wore. We dreamed about synthetics. That was a new kind of goods that was durable, among other virtues. All of us sometimes banded together to get the five meters allotted per person, because no one alone could stand that many hours in the lines that started forming at night for this synthetic goods.

A nice, very quiet girl named Galya lived with us. Sometimes we'd get her some of this synthetic goods or other hard-to-get wares out of sympathy and respect for her demanding job. She worked at night, at very responsible and highly secret work. We weren't supposed to know what she did, but we knew, though we never talked about it. Galya worked on the radio-jamming station that was in the same building as our Institute. She had trouble with her studies, particularly Marxism-Leninism. Galya was not very articulate, being a country girl and not well educated. She sent everything she earned to her family on the kolkhoz, spending hardly anything on herself. Her job exhausted her. Three times a week, she would set the alarm for 3:00 A.M., wake up, get dressed quietly, trying to make no noise, grunting occasionally, and whispering something. She'd drink a glass of warm tea, wrap herself in her old, loose, country-style overcoat, tie on a thick, countrified shawl, and leave. Sometimes I'd meet Galya on the stairs when I was coming back from seeing Oleg at the radio station, and she'd smile dolefully and murmur, "I'm going on foot to save taxi fare, I still have time."

"And what happens if you're late?"

"Don't say that, don't, I can't be a single second late ever, Lord save us!"

"And can't you take a nap there? Just doze off a little?"

Galya smiled at me as if I were a child.

"You know what they could do if I did. And anyway,

I wouldn't be able to sleep for fear. Well, go on to bed now, you haven't much sleeptime left either."

We felt very sorry for Galya. Knowing how important and secret her work was, we never questioned her, though I was very curious to know what she jammed. At first I didn't know what radio jamming was, but Rita explained it to me. She and Galya were both in fourth year.

"It's a special installation that works on the same principle as any radio station except it broadcasts noise to jam other stations."

"What's the point of jamming them?"

"I don't know and don't want to know."

"But, Rita, it costs so much money! The noise broadcast has to be louder than the voices of the station. How much power do they have to use? We studied that in radio technology."

"We did, too. But if they do it, it means it's necessary. That's all. And I don't want to talk about it ever again."

We sympathized with Galya silently, realizing how important it was not to let something harmful get into the air.

We had another country girl, Masha; from Smolensk Province. Masha was very talkative and given to occasional fits of anger. Her record was spoiled because she had been in occupied territory. Whenever we had to fill out forms, and that happened several times during the school year, Masha would start crying and get mad.

"I've filled out so many of these forms already, over and over again. And every time, there's the same punch line: 'What were you doing during the occupation?' What was I doing, yes, what was I doing? I wasn't doing anything—except digging up potatoes with Mother, looking after my sister, and starving. Besides, I was all of twelve years old during that wretched occupation. And as for the Germans, bad as they may be, I never laid eyes on one in our village, yet my whole life's ruined."

Of all my roommates, Rita was the only one to launch into polemics.

"What's the matter with you? You can't trust everyone. Maybe the Germans gave you a mission of some kind."

"Sure, sure, at the age of twelve! Besides, I don't know a single German, I tell you, the Germans just went through our village and we never saw them again. Oh, girls, how evil we all are. The people in my village are so warm and trusting, but when I came to the city I became like a chained dog myself, the same as Rita here with her 'You can't trust everyone.' Sometimes I just shake with anger and burst into tears for no good reason, I'm so hurt by human injustice, evil, and mistrust. And the young men here are so coarse and insistent, trying to steal a girl's honor. In the village, no one even wanted to look at me, I was so thin, but here, sailors and soldiers pursue me right on the street, proposing all sorts of improper things. I keep on my guard because I keep thinking maybe someone from the city will marry me and I won't have to go back and starve. But city men are used to fast girls, there's only one thing they want. They even call you bad names when you refuse."

Masha was beautiful. She had a narrow, elegant face with chiseled features, and her thick, wavy hair and strangely light brown eyes with dark flecks added to her appeal. She had no figure, though. She was bony, with angular, sloping shoulders, crooked, skinny fingers, and no curves at all. Her legs were skinny, too, a bit crooked, and unused to high heels, which gave her an unnatural, half-loping gait. No one ever sent Masha anything. Her scholarship barely allowed for a scanty fare, but Masha economized on that, too, because she was saving for the wardrobe she considered absolutely essential for catching

a city husband. Sometimes when Masha sat down at
the table with her invariable bowl of pea soup, she would
philosophize.

"Why brood about it? Your stomach just gets wind
and you're just as hungry. And you're still as bony as
a sorry kolkhoz nag. Men throw themselves at a face
like flies and turn up their noses at the rest. The fools,
they think that's where happiness lies. In the village,
the lazy leeches look for bit tits and fat behinds. And
these, here in town, look for a figure, a Mam'selle with
a swinging behind and suggestive glances. But no decent
man has come along yet, only my little fool, who really
seems to love me, but there's no making kasha with
him—they won't let him marry me because he's a
foreigner. He says he loves me and wants to marry me,
he even kissed my hand. He's a fine fellow, good-looking,
and he says his father is a doctor back home, which means
they must live well. That's just what I needed—what
a pity he's a foreigner."

The boy was actually very nice. Tall, handsome, well
educated, and obviously truly in love with Masha. They
often used to stand in the dormitory corridor at night
and spring away from each other whenever a door banged
anywhere.

Masha had complaints about him, too:

"Foreigners are no better than our own male dogs.
Yesterday he pestered and pestered me so, I almost had
to slap him to quiet him. He hugged and kissed me,
then started pressing closer and closer and breathing
heavily like a wild beast, and he turned red and started
trembling. I was very afraid something would happen,
he's strong as an ox, you see, I couldn't cope with him
in a million years. But I was lucky, someone went to
the bathroom and he jumped away. He was still shaking
a long time after, and then he started telling me he
couldn't go on like this, after all, that he was flesh and

blood, not a stick of wood, and we'd been standing in the corridor a whole year already and I still wouldn't go to his room. He said he could arrange it so none of the fellows were there and we could be alone together for once. When I asked, 'What for?' he laughed and said when people love each other, they don't just spend the nights standing in the corridor. I understood right away, but just to hear what he'd say, I said, 'And who will marry me after that?' He laughed harder and said no one paid any attention to that anymore. Then I lost my temper and blurted out, 'Where I live, they do. And I don't live *there*, I live *here*, and please take that into account, my good sir.' Can you imagine, girls? He was offended. He said good-bye, just kissed me on the cheek, and left. Looking so sad."

They broke up for good over a funny thing. Our Masha was not noted for her sense of humor. The disagreement took place in our room when we were sitting having supper together on our pooled resources, Masha's foreigner, too. Suddenly he said, jokingly, "Girls, this is my sixth year of studying Russian and I still haven't mastered the fine points. Please explain this to me. If a girl is called Galya for short, her full name is Galina; if she's Polya, then it's Polina. And if it's Masha, shouldn't her full name be Mashina*?"

We laughed. Masha scowled.

"Mashenka, are you my *mashina* then? Light or heavy? Or perhaps a diesel? Masha, the diesel from Gorki Auto Factory, Masha-GAF."

That was too much. Masha leaned across the table.

"Ah, you shameless foreign clown. He has such a silly name himself, my good people, yet he sneers at a good Russian one. I'm embarrassed to introduce him to people, I can't write home about who my friend is,

*Mashina* is the Russian word for "truck."

they'd be afraid he's some kind of beast. Ishtvan! Girls, it takes nerve to laugh at other names with one like that. *Eesh*tvan [she mispronounced it deliberately, though she knew very well it was *Ish*tvan], why it's impossible to say, it twists your tongue in two. For your information, Eeshtvan, my name is Maria. And I'll show you a *mashina* that'll make you forget the way to our room. Out, you foreign leech!"

Shouting, sobbing, Masha jumped on the frightened, humiliated young man and began beating him with her fists. After she drove him out, everyone felt awkward, but Masha kept on reviling the man's parents for giving their son such a good-for-nothing name that it was embarrassing to say it out loud in front of people. She reviled him, too, saying he was neither fish nor fowl, certainly nothing to write home about.

And since she couldn't marry him anyway, it was a good thing she'd driven the fool out.

They broke up then. But several years later, when I came back from Siberia after Stalin had died and Khrushchev was in power, I learned that Masha and Ishtvan had gotten married, and that he had taken her back to Hungary with him.

Oleg was graduated with honors. They let him stay in Leningrad, working at the same address he had before, but a serious problem presented itself—where to live? He was asked to leave the dormitory as soon as he had finished defending his thesis. We walked over the whole city, even took buses to the outskirts, asked janitors, workers, anybody and everybody if they knew where there might be a room or a corner of one for rent. The rest of the time, we went to the movies and just walked around, since I'd stayed in Leningrad for the winter recess in order to be with Oleg. Besides, I had no place to go.

During a film, I'd often glance at Oleg and wonder

what he was thinking about. He always watched the
screen very seriously, stroked my hand, and paid no
attention at all to my grunting and snorting. We always
left the movie in silence. Later that made me wonder.
After all, a film ought to arouse some controversy: One
can like or not like a film. But we were silent. We had
nothing to say. We should have reacted, but that was
impossible—that took words, and we were afraid of
words. If anyone had dared say how bad, how false the
films were, he'd have to say the same about books, pictures, yes, about every aspect of life. I knew what village
life was like from Masha. I knew how Galina's family
lived. I knew about Siberia, there's a lot I myself could
have told about our own existence there. But on the
screen, they showed jolly kolkhozes, songs, and dances.
You'd think all they ever did was sit at long tables proposing toasts and offering congratulations, drinking wine,
and eating suckling pig with buckwheat kasha. There
were heroes in the factories, heroes in the schools, heroes
on the kolkhozes. Nothing but heroes. Where were the
people? Where were the problems? That forced cheerful-
ness made everything false and depressing. There was
nothing to say. That probably explains why, when the
Tarzan series appeared in movie houses, there were huge
lines for tickets and students skipped classes because at
the Barricade Cinema around the corner the tickets were
cheaper during the day. I must say I remember Chita
the chimpanzee's pranks in *Tarzan* better than the heroic
events or even the subject of any other film of that time.
The most I remember is a well-performed excerpt from
a Tchaikovsky concerto and a ridiculous rosy suckling
pig on a platter in the center of a table heaped with good
things to eat—this when the kolkhozniks from surround-
ing villages were coming to Leningrad to buy bread, and
people were still standing in long lines for it in Siberia.
It was the same with books—they left nothing but

a bad taste. They were false, false throughout, cheery, contrived, colorless. All were made according to the unvarying formula of the kitchen that concocted the plays and the films that covered entire walls with huge, vulgar, characterless pictures of smiling steelworkers, or of Stalin's eagles downing Hitler's rash aces or our leaders sunk deep in radiant thought. Everything was so thoroughly worked out that there was nothing to discuss. We were spared the trouble of thinking. Everything was fine, just as it should be. We made the recipes, we cook; you eat and sing the praises. Some praised, we were silent. And many were silent. Did they realize it was all lies? I don't know. It made me uneasy. At the time, I was glad Oleg was silent, too, but later on, when I met him in Siberia and I couldn't keep still anymore, he was as silent as ever. As for me, life had changed me; my mind had stopped accepting poison from that false kitchen. But at the time we were very much in love.

There were no rooms to be had. Oleg found a corner in a room with the landlady and her daughter, age twenty. They were obviously pinning their hopes on the charms of the daughter and the flimsiness of the cotton curtain dividing Oleg's corner from the daughter's bed. We used to exchange hasty kisses in the bathroom, but we couldn't linger there. It was a large, communal apartment, and the lodgers always started pounding on the door.

In spring, it was simpler; one could wander around the city. Oleg could walk a long time in the dead of winter, but the toes and fingers I had frozen in Siberia always started to get frostbite right away. We searched for deserted corners, but where were we to find them in a city of so many homeless lovers? They were building a stadium near the Tuchkov Bridge. We usually met there, I coming from Vassilievsky, Oleg from Petrogradsky.

Oleg sometimes became exasperated. "I don't see why you insist on this aimless way of living. We're both wasting time and patience on these so-called excursions. Why are you so against our getting married?"

But I loved Oleg, and I knew marrying me would ruin his life. He had just started his career, and his life was not an easy one either. His father had died at the front, his mother had had to bring him up with his little sister by herself. Oleg studied and worked all year. Once connected with me, he couldn't even dream of a career in the field of science. He was extremely ambitious and obviously talented, since he had been taken on as a post-graduate student in Leningrad immediately after leaving the Institute. I don't think he ever gave a thought to what it would cost him to marry a Jew. And as for the rest, he had never even guessed at it.

I usually dismissed his arguments with a joke. Sometimes I would argue back.

"What does it matter if somebody looks askance at us! They're such bigots. It doesn't bother me if some fool of a woman doesn't speak to me because I'm 'loose.'"

"It bothers me."

"There's no reason. Look, if you and I can find a real room with a door of its own, instead of this wretched corner behind a cupboard, I'll move in with you altogether and no one will know we're not married. Our mothers are far away and why should we inform strangers? No one's going to ask us for our wedding certificate!"

"They will, of course they will. You can't rent a room for two without a wedding certificate. You can't go any-where on vacation without it, they won't let you in a hotel. Let's assume I rent a room and you move in. If there's one single neighbor who doesn't like your using the bathroom or being in the kitchen, we'll have a fine to pay at the militia for breaking the passport laws. And you won't be protected from disgrace either. They'll call your place of work. Besides, this is the first time I've heard of a girl not wanting to get married. Maybe you have some special reason. Then you might let me in on it, as a somewhat interested person."

We began quarreling, parted "forever," loved one another again, and my constant anxiety, my always being on guard, subtly influenced Oleg. Without knowing anything concrete, he sensed it was for his sake I didn't want us to be officially connected.

I passed my second-year exams with great success, with two or three *fours*. The hated courses in mathematics, strength of materials, and other theoretical, technical intricacies were done with; they had passed by, uncomprehended and unappreciated.

Oleg went to visit his mother in central Russia, and I joined him there after my exams. That summer was the happiest of my life.

From the big railway junction on the Moscow–Vladivostok line where Oleg met me, we took a bus to a fairly small suburb where we had to change once again to get to his mother's house. But we had missed the last bus and had to spend the night. With some difficulty, we found a woman who gave up her own bed and went to spend the night in the hayloft. We walked around the suburb a while, admiring the stars. Oleg told me about places nearby. For the first time, we felt truly together. We were unable to sleep for a long while from happiness. Exactly half a year later, I was to find myself in this suburb once again.

It was hard to believe. A month without problems, without irritations. A month of constant, peaceful, tangible happiness. Oleg's mother treated me wisely and kindly, never asked any questions, gave no advice, just accepted me as if I were a member of the family. I was very grateful because her tact, unusual in a Party member and a person who held a very responsible post, spared me those unpleasant and dangerous conversations that might have exposed my dark past . . . and present . . . and, of course, future.

Our mornings began with a discussion of what to do—pick mushrooms or berries, fish, or just take an excursion on foot or by bicycle. We used to go after mushrooms with lots of special equipment: jars strung on a rope for the tiny saffron milk-cap mushrooms used in marinades; a pail for the real, white mushrooms, edible boletus, of which we picked only the young; a rucksack for brown-cap and orange-cap boletus to fry. We brought back pails of raspberries and bilberries, too. It was there I learned how to make jam and keep house in general. I never learned to milk goats, though—I always felt milking was painful for them, and I was a little frightened in the dark shed. When Oleg's mother left for town for a few days and entrusted the goats to me, the first time I milked them the beasts ate the lantern I had carelessly left within their reach—glass and all. When I heard the crunch of glass under the goats' teeth in pitch darkness, I froze in terror. The goats grunted with triumph, their green eyes glittering, but Oleg brought them to order very skillfully.

Fishing was my greatest joy. Just a kilometer from the house flowed a river, not very deep, not very swift, winding, and fairly broad. They floated wood down it in springtime, and here and there you could see barricades to trap logs. That was where the fish were. To the amazement of Oleg, who considered me impossibly restless, I would sit for hours with a rod trying to outsmart the smart chub. But chub are cautious fish. They moved in rather small schools, and it's as if they saw me through the transparent, sunlit water between the boulders along the shore and the log barricades. I used to pick out the fattest chub, dangle the hook with a fly right under its nose, sometimes touching the fish right on the head with the bait, but he would refuse it as if making fun of me. River perch, on the other hand, would swallow a worm at once, hook and all. We also caught heaps of tiny gudgeon, which Oleg's mother used to drench in flour and fry. We ate them like sunflower seeds.

Burbot was our staple catch, however. Oleg used to wade chest-deep or even swim under water, harpoon in hand, to spot a burbot moored to the bottom. Fat as a pig, the burbot usually stays motionless at the bottom of the river, nose into the current, barely moving its tail. On sighting his prey, Oleg would lead the burbot onto what we called "operating territory" with well-aimed pokes of the harpoon, and there we'd catch him. I would walk along the bank with a pail, knee-deep in water, acting as stevedore. Sometimes I'd fish out a small burbot with just an ordinary fork. I don't know if burbot are as lazy everywhere as they are in central Russia. I used to grumble about the pail being too heavy, but the next morning we'd have a delicious-smelling pastry stuffed with burbot liver waiting for us for breakfast.

One event seemed truly like a dream. I was sitting deep in thought on the edge of a brightly sunlit clearing in the woods. Suddenly, out leaped a squirrel. He walked up and down comically, rose up on his hind paws, looked around the clearing very attentively, and seemed to whistle. As if dumped out of a sack, six or seven funny, reddish, fluffy little squirrels spilled out into the clearing and sat down in a row. The mama squirrel—or perhaps it was the papa—walked gravely up and down in front of them as if holding a military drill before battle. Some of the little ones sat peacefully; some raised themselves on their hind legs, swaying and touching their little noses with their front paws, and sometimes they would leave the formation in twos and threes and perform what was obviously an exercise, though mysterious to me. I watched, bewitched.

All at once, something devilish got into me. With a

yelp, I rushed forward, tearing off my jacket as I went.
When I threw the jacket at the little squirrels I noticed
the mother was the first to escape. The baby squirrels
scattered in all directions, except for two that stayed under
the jacket. In excitement, I put my hand in, wanting
to pet them. Oh! How hard they bit! Two of my fingers
felt as if they'd had needles driven into them. Oleg came
running when I yelled. We had a rather stormy discussion
about the fate of the little squirrels, which Oleg said would
be destroyed pitilessly if left here because there was a
special office where you could get five rubles per skin.
Those five rubles determined my squirrels' fate. I decided
to keep them.

Squirrel bites take a long time to heal. The little ones
often bit me, every time I tried to make friends, but by
the end of the summer, they were used to both Oleg's
mother and me. They drank milk from a saucer like kittens
and sat up comically on their hind legs to nibble seeds
and nuts. I used to bring them pine cones. Once I forgot
to close the cage and the squirrels disappeared. That
evening, when Oleg and I were sitting on a bench in
front of the house, we heard a familiar clucking noise
and our little squirrels hopped up on my shoulder as
they were used to doing.

We left them with Oleg's mother. We couldn't find
enough living space in Leningrad for ourselves, let alone
two squirrels. His mother used to write about their pranks
in detail, and the following summer, when I was in
Siberia, I got a letter from Oleg in which he wrote that
the squirrels had run away, this time for good, when
he forgot to close the cage.

I had to be in Leningrad by the first of September.
Oleg went ahead a few days earlier to look for a room
and he had unbelievable luck. He found a room for rent
in a fairly small apartment with four families in it. The

room was tiny, eight square meters, but it had space
for a bed, a table, and a chair. A clothesline on which
he hung his shirts and only jacket served as his closet.
True, the door to the room opened into the kitchen, from
which you could hear the quietest conversation, to say
nothing of the housewives shouting. But the real problem
was a crazy woman who lived in the apartment. She
was a plump, very good-looking, serious, well-educated
young woman, studying for an advanced degree in
philosophy. Her mother said it was love that had driven
her mad. She used to lie in wait for Oleg in the kitchen,
and if he didn't get away in time, he would be bombarded
by threats mixed with love prattle and quotations from
dialectical materialism. Oleg was afraid of her, and I was
even more so; she saw me as the fairy-tale witch who
separates lovers.

I usually stayed with Oleg from Saturday to Sunday
and slept in the dormitory all week where, this time,
they had assigned me with girls in the same year, but
from another field. Again we were six, all quite different
from one another. One, Nadya, was a Party member.
A close friend of hers, an Estonian, was like me in that
she never mentioned her parents. One girl from near
Novosibirsk became a very good friend of mine. (She
was, incidentally, the only one who dared tell Oleg everything that had happened that night after my disappearance. She even enclosed a very friendly note to me
in one of Oleg's letters.)

We all got on well and used to organize collective
suppers of hot potatoes and herring and sometimes even
wine, if guests were invited. We organized what we
dubbed "cultural expeditions" to the baths, too.
Sometimes we had long talks about life. We had started
thinking about where we would be assigned, though it
was still three years off. Our first practical work lay ahead
of us. Some were being sent to a factory in Riga for practi-

cal work. When we filled out forms at the beginning of the school year, I was afraid to mention I'd been born in Riga for fear someone might wonder why, in that case, my mother was in Siberia. Everyone believed my story that my family had remained in Siberia after being evacuated.

We were kept very busy with new, specialized subjects and much more laboratory work than before. I found it fascinating and sometimes felt technology was not only for the chosen after all. I particularly liked puttering with the soldering iron, and loved the smell of resin.

Our Party member, Nadya, sometimes reproved me for my lack of interest in socially useful work. She took part at Party, Komsomol, and other such meetings, and rounded up unpublic-spirited people like me for all sorts of voluntary work on Sundays. Nadya often had to prepare lectures on "The International Situation" and reports on technical subjects. We had newspapers in the room for the first time because Nadya made extracts. We turned on the radio only to check the time or smile sarcastically during weather forecasts (we often had rain instead of the sun that was announced). This, of course, was the only area in which criticism was permitted.

I was very close to Lyalya as before. We often doubledated, I with Oleg and Lyalya with her friend, who was waiting for a divorce in order to marry her. When I had told her of my relations with Oleg, she had cried over my fallen honor and lost purity, sobbed, stroked my head and hands, and said how important it was to keep one's self intact until marriage. Exactly three months later, Lyalya, again sobbing, told me she was pregnant. Having a child was impossible under the circumstances, and abortions were forbidden, but she said that her lover had promised to find a doctor who would do an abortion in strict secrecy for a large sum. Would I be kind enough

to meet her after the abortion and bring her home to
the dormitory?

I froze on the street for three hours. When I saw
Lyalya, I hardly recognized her. Her face was gray,
lifeless, and wore a strange expression. In the taxi, she
whispered she would not wish such fear, pain, and shame
on her worst enemy. It seems it all took place on the
table in a kitchen shared by the two families in the apartment, and that the operation had to be done in a hurry
before the other lodgers got back from work. There was
no anesthetic and she was not allowed to groan because
it might be heard in the stairway. The doctor warned
her they'd both go to prison if caught. The operation
cost Lyalya three months' scholarship money, but she
got more money from home by telling her parents some
lies.

Some years later Oleg told me how Lyalya cried when
she learned of my disappearance, but when he asked
her if she wanted to write me, she said her parents
wouldn't allow her to have any contact whatsoever with
me. She apologized by explaining it could endanger her
father's position as political worker in the army.

Mama suddenly displayed anxiety in her letters. She
wrote that Father had traveled through Kansk without
her seeing him and was now to live permanently somewhere not far from our former village of Dzerzhinsk.
She wrote in allusions and incomplete sentences, but
I had learned how to decipher her letters. There was
something quite unpleasant in her last one: "Do you
remember our neighbor Rosa's naughty son Lev? Well,
the madcap—he'd gone away to live with relatives about
the same time you did—just disappeared not long ago.
Imagine, the rascal, and Rosa doesn't even know where
he is. But Irochka came home to her mother's not long

ago. She dropped her studies at the Institute in Moscow in her third year and was delighted to see her mother again. Perhaps you'll come back too?"

I understood all too well. That "rascal" Lev and Irochka were both, like me, children of exiles who had gone to live with relatives as youngsters. Mother was telling me Lev had been arrested and put in prison, while Ira, realizing she faced the same fate, had preferred to return voluntarily to her mother in Siberia. It was a rather threatening message.

But when you are nineteen, how can you believe anything bad will happen to you? Especially if you're as happy as I was. Oleg never read Mama's letters, but he knew from my mood when I'd gotten one. Sometimes he asked what my Mama was doing, or my sister, but he understood from my curt replies that it was better not to ask. He was a little offended. His own mother used to send love to both of us in her letters.

Our lecturer on Marxism-Leninism hanged himself in the bathroom at the Institute. There was no obituary, no funeral. A teacher in the department of vacuum equipment suddenly disappeared, and another, from the department of electrical machinery. Two students vanished without a trace, one from the town, the other from the dormitory, a fifth-year student. No one asked any questions. If someone disappeared, it was because that was the way it had to be.

# Act IV*

## JOURNEY FROM LENINGRAD TO SIBERIA

A R R E S T

Oleg and I said good-bye at the entrance to my dormitory after arranging to meet the following morning at the Moscow Station, where his mother was to arrive. He took with him the skates I'd just bought; the rink was closer to his house. Happy and frozen—it was the beginning of December—I rushed into the warm vestibule, noticing as I did a stranger sitting at the house porter's desk. "Handsome fellow, not one of us, not a student," I thought. How astonished I was when he suddenly addressed me, not by my surname, but as "citizeness." Quite civilly, he asked me to come with him into a small room I had never noticed before, right next to the porter's desk. The moment the door closed behind us, he held out a paper to me and growled, with no longer a trace of civility:

"You're under arrest. Here's the order. Read it. Understood? That's that. Try not to act hysterical, it won't help. Now we'll go quietly up to your room. It's being searched. You will speak to no one on the way. Walk as if nothing had happened. Then you'll come with us."

"Where?"

*This part was written in 1953 in exile.

153

"You'll see." And, looking at my face, he added, "No questions. It's clear enough."

That was *it*. For eleven years, since the night the bell rang so long, so terrifyingly, and they took us away to Siberia, I had known no peace. It was a legacy from Mother, who had never known peace since that hour either, and was always waiting for *something* to happen. *What,* she didn't know, but something bad. That "something will explode" was firmly and deeply implanted in me, too, but it hadn't kept me from enjoying life, falling in love, laughing, dancing to oblivion, and generally being happy except for that gnawing little wormhole. The worm that lived in me often slept, but liked to remind me of its existence in my happiest moments so that I wouldn't be carried away. It would give me a stab in the heart—and go back to sleep. Just to remind me of how vulnerable I was.

But one's nature is such that I laughed all the same, enjoyed myself all the same, became impassioned, and fell in love. And when *it* came at last in the form of a handsome young man with an order for my arrest in his hands, I didn't feel so frightened. *It* had come, that's all—hello there.

My dormitory room was on the third floor. Men were searching it, in deep silence, while my friends sat around the table with discomfited faces. The contents of my nightstand had been turned out on the table. My suitcase, which I kept under my bed, had also been ransacked. Panties, brassieres, and towels were strewn over the bed. The bed was turned inside out. "My Lord, what are they looking for? As if I were a criminal!"

Two men were rifling through my things. It looked so indecent, particularly those brassieres strewn on the bed, that I felt naked, humiliated. My throat tightened; tears came. I swallowed hard, but they kept flowing, which was even more humiliating.

"Gather your things together and get dressed. No,

no. No notes, no oral instructions, no talking. Your things will be in the car. Leave and go downstairs as if going out for a walk. With no talking. That's all. Get moving."

They took my passport, Komsomol card, student record book, notebook, letters, and all sorts of papers; my money too, to the last kopeck. One of my three escorts carried my things while I set out for a walk with the other two, quietly, without hysterics, as instructed.

"Good-bye, girls!" I said uncertainly in the doorway. No one answered. They just sat around the table with discomfited faces, as if stunned. That hurt me. We had lived in such close friendship, sharing even our grants in a common pot.

A little to one side of the entrance to the dorm was a gray Pobeda. We drove off.

We drove through marvelous places. I stared eagerly at the sphinxes brought back from ancient Egypt, at the University that had inhospitably closed its doors to me, at the frozen Neva under the Palace Bridge, at the silhouette of my beloved Fortress of Peter and Paul, at Saint Isaac's Cathedral, all illuminated, and the glittering spire of the Admiralty Building. Across the bridge, we turned left. How strangely man is made, I thought. He's taken the devil knows where, perhaps to be shot, perhaps to be imprisoned for life, and he admires the city. And what was my handsome companion thinking, I'd like to know? Did he love Leningrad? On the little bridge over the canal by the Summer Garden, the thought "You'll never see this again!" suddenly pierced me with pain.

I knew by now where I was being taken: to the Big House on Liteiny Street. It was a house of terror. People went out of their way to avoid walking past it, the windows were lit all night, and while still a child in Siberia, I'd heard it was a place from which no one returned, like the Lubyanka in Moscow.

My fellow passengers were silent. I shed inner tears

for Leningrad, for Oleg. How would he find out? What would he think? They wouldn't tell him I was a criminal, would they? Yet there was nothing to say! Tomorrow, his mother would arrive. He'd be angry at first at not finding me at the station, and think I'd overslept. Then they'd both start worrying. And call the dormitory, where someone would mutter something incomprehensible —why, no one there knew any more than I did. How will he live without me now? And I without him? Would I live at all? Oh, when I'm only nineteen? What are they doing to me?

Many, many sad thoughts overwhelmed me at last, but I didn't cry. Only, in my throat and a bit lower down, it felt as if someone were grasping my tightened cords and wrapping them tighter and tighter until it hurt to breathe. That was just as bad, I felt, as tears. A stream of hot water was about to gush from my eyes. Glancing out the corner of my eye at my handsome escort, I caught his look. It almost seemed sympathetic. Suddenly, completely unexpectedly, and only to keep the tears back, I said loudly:

"What kind of work is this of yours? Is this your job—arresting people like me who aren't guilty of anything?"

Perhaps I'd only imagined the sympathy in his eyes, perhaps not, but now they turned to stone.

"So you turn out to be a philosopher! It's not for nothing you were arrested, then."

Imagine! He knew it was for nothing, you see, but if I proved to be a philosopher, that was reason enough. I thought he should have been arrested for such an explanation.

I had no time to reply. The car drove up to the high black gates of the Big House itself, not from Liteiny, but from the other side, Voinov Street. The gates opened noiselessly at once and the car entered as if sliding through a lock. They closed just as noiselessly behind us. Ahead appeared a second set, exactly like the first. These opened, let us through, closed, and we were in the inner prison. It was night.


## THE HOUSE OF TERROR

The sentry checked the papers at length and said something to my escorts in a low voice. He couldn't turn me over to men, of course, he explained, and the women were very busy; we would have to wait. My escorts were displeased and tired. Then a woman in a white smock appeared and led me into an adjoining room. Another one, obviously a nurse, came in. They ordered me to undress.

"Things on the chair."

I took off my clothes one by one, stopping to look expectantly at them each time.

"All of it, all of it, get a move on!"

I stood naked. Their attentive inspection was disagreeable. They talked together softly and wrote something down, glancing at me. The nurse came up, raised my hands, looked in my mouth, and touched my head for some reason.

My lord! It seems I'd held back something of importance; there were ribbons entwined in my braids, and a few hairpins.

"Unbraid the braids. Hairpins and ribbons on the chair." (Later on it was explained to me that one could hang oneself with ribbons.)

In the corner stood a heavy wire cage. They put me in it, ordered me to stand on a chair. There I stood, naked, with my hair loose. "Lorelei in the zoo," flashed across my mind, but I felt miserable on this pedestal under these unfriendly eyes.

After fumbling with my things, they handed them to me one by one through a little window in the cage and ordered me to dress, balancing right there on the chair.

All the elastic had been removed from the panties and girdle; the skirt had no fasteners, nor did the sweater. Nothing would stay on. It was terribly awkward moving around like that. They didn't give me back the ribbons either. Why did I listen to Oleg and not cut off my braids? I'd wanted to cut my hair so badly, but he liked to bury his face in that thick shock. He should see me now.

The procedure was over. The women turned me over to a guard who led me down endless corridors and stairways lined with a strip of soft carpeting. We walked a long time. At last, on one of the upper floors, we turned a corner—Halt! There was a door with a three-digit number. It opened, let me through, closed. No one.

I glanced around. The cell was quite decent. Left of the door, a cot; on it, a mattress, a pillow, a thin blanket. All were covered with revolting stains. A washstand and a latrine bucket stood in one corner. Right under the ceiling was the tiniest window. It was only the following morning that I noticed a shield in front of the window blocked all but the narrowest strip of sky. Even that was an advantage, as I realized later when I was in cells where even this strip did not exist. An electric bulb burned over the door. That was all.

I stood there in the middle of the cell. A little window in the door opened and a man's voice said, "Lie down!"

I lay down. Sleep would not come. My thoughts galloped on as if possessed, disconnected and strange. Thoughts of exams, my record book, the girls' faces, and Father—all at once, I was interested in knowing what he felt when he was arrested. I remembered he, too, had cried. All my thoughts ended with Oleg, tomorrow morning. And all the time, I kept wanting to cry. It was hard to breathe. I found relief in whimpering softly so the knot in my throat would not be so tight. I felt deeply hurt.

"Why is this happening to me? Whom have I harmed? Is it because of Papa? If it's true they gave him ten years for a stupid question, for some sort of anecdote, we didn't both tell it! Why me? I, who've been in the Komsomol since I was thirteen and taken on so many Party tasks. I was even secretary of a Komsomol organization with several hundred members. They were always all satisfied. And I was doing well in school, I'd turned over a new leaf in the Institute, was getting almost straight *fives*. Then why? Am I supposed to be living in exile like Mama? But I left entirely legally, I didn't run off, and furthermore, I was only thirteen. I wasn't even old enough to be on the special records. Perhaps they found out I'd lied on questionnaires? Then they'd throw me out of the Institute and that would be the end of it. There had been cases like that. But here I am in solitary in the Big House. What for? For being Jewish? I haven't heard of anyone being imprisoned for that alone yet. And we weren't exiled for that either. There were lots of Latvians, Russians, and Germans along with us. And lots of exiled Lithuanians, Ukrainians, and even Chinese lived in Siberia and all the Volga Germans were sent there. True, they wouldn't let me in the University for that reason in spite of my medal . . . Could a new law have come out to imprison people for that? It's possible. Or has somebody informed against me? But there's no one likely. I never talked politics with anyone and no one talked politics in front of me. Even Oleg and I never talked about anything of that kind. He knows nothing about me. How ridiculous! Now, why didn't I tell him something, at least? He'd feel better now, he wouldn't be thinking I'm a criminal."

Perhaps I'd been accused of espionage? Perhaps my

superior knowledge of German looked suspicious? What a fool I was not to put on a better act. Of course I'd distorted the pronunciation badly, but I might have been too lax sometimes, and here was the consequence. Here I was in the Big House, where they only keep political prisoners.

Then came terror.

"What's going to happen to me now? Prison, hard labor for life? And what of Oleg, and my life, and the Institute?" But through the chaos and fear, one thought persisted—"Don't cry over the inevitable." What good would tears do me, or self-pity and moaning about my life being ruined? Thoughts like that only made things harder. One must just take oneself in hand and say, "There's nothing terrifying and no shame of any kind. Let the guilty feel ashamed. And one must sleep in order to stay cheerful. Anyway, the best thing is to pretend this isn't happening to me, that I'm seeing it in a movie." And all at once the thought "like in a movie" made me feel better. I even began feeling sleepy.

The bell rang. Problems of the present absorbed me completely, such as how to keep my skirt from falling down and what to do with my hair—I could hardly go around looking like a mermaid. It would be nice to cut it, but I had nothing to cut with. Suddenly I saw a little crack of light in the door. "They're peeping! They should be ashamed! How am I to get up? Why, it might be a man!"

Heavens, how naïve I was on my first day. It was the usual peephole, and it was there to be looked through. The guard in the corridor was just doing his duty.

"Get up! Reveille at six. Violations mean the punishment cell. We have a regime here. Wash, dress, relieve yourself. No lying down, no sitting on the bed until lights out. Violations mean the punishment cell. Sit on the chair to the right of the door, facing the door. Move the table and chair out from the wall in the daytime; put them back at night. Walking around the cell is permitted, talking is not. Lights out at eleven. Get up! Obey!"

The fool, couldn't he see I was embarrassed to get up while he was watching? The shutter had closed. Had he understood?

I did everything as ordered, though I was very afraid he might look in while I was relieving myself. Once that was over with, I put the chair and table in their appointed place. It's strange I hadn't noticed them before. And how lucky I was to be thin! The chair was a narrow metal slat, the table not much bigger. I sat down. Oh, but the metal was cold! I felt sleepy. I took the pillow from the bed to put under my head, but no, no, none of your tricks, my dear—"No sleeping during the day. Taking the pillow or blanket from the bed is forbidden. Violations mean the punishment cell."

I remembered walking around the cell was permitted. Thanks for that. I walked. I counted the steps. To the window, first seven, then eight steps, and the same back. From the bed to the table—three steps. One could walk on the diagonal and around the perimeter, too, but it became boring quickly. And I was hungry and sleepy.

The train has probably already arrived. His mother won't ask why I'm not there, but Oleg will be furious! "On a day like this, she could have woken up in time!" Then he'll telephone. Will he tell her anything? He's so reticent, and, after all, his mother is a Party member. To have her son connected with a political criminal! But she's a very intelligent woman, she has such penetrating eyes. I complained to Oleg one day that when she looked at me, I felt she knew not only what I was thinking then, but what I'd been thinking the day before. He laughed and said, "My mother is very smart, that's why she doesn't say much."

She would be unhappy for his sake. And as for

him—oh, my poor, abandoned darling! Such a wave of
pity and tenderness for Oleg swept over me that I suddenly burst into loud crying, sobbing, choking. But not
for long. The peephole opened. I had time to think, "This
must be forbidden, too—violations mean the punishment
cell. Well, I won't cry in front of you, I'll show you."
I turned my back to the door and began whistling. That
was a violation, too, it seems.

"No singing, no whistling, no talking. Violations
mean the punishment cell."

Oh, the beasts, there are so many things forbidden.
Who was I disturbing? And the fools with their "no
talking." Who would I talk to? Myself?

The day dragged on endlessly. Three times they
brought me food, which they handed through the little
window in the door. The first time, they brought a piece
of bread, a fairly big one. I ate it up with pleasure. Later,
I found out it was the entire daily ration. They also
brought a mugful of warm slop—coffee—and not quite
a teaspoonful of sugar, wrapped in a piece of cloth. For
dinner, I got a full bowl of some sort of cloudy liquid
with fish scales swimming on top. It smelled bad, but
I was starving and gulped the first spoonful briskly. Oof!
I was nauseated at once. I had to pour the soup into
the latrine bucket.

"Finding food disagreeable means the punishment
cell!"

Now there's one for you, you couldn't even refuse
to eat. The idea of calling it food, too, the devils. But
when I handed the bowl through the little window, a
pleasant male voice gave me some friendly advice.

"Pretend you're eating, and as soon as he's gone,
pour it into the latrine bucket, quickly."

I wanted to thank him, but the window banged shut.

Well, well, so there are human beings even here. I
felt warmer inside.

That evening, they brought a mug of warm tea which I had to drink without sugar. It seems I had exhausted my daily ration of less than a teaspoon in the morning. With the tea came half a bowl of cold, lumpy kasha. I found it delicious. At eleven, the ringing of the bell, and lights out. Oh, how endlessly it had dragged by, that first day in prison. I couldn't believe I could lie down on the bed without being shouted at. My thoughts still galloped about a little. Phrases that had seemed pat before were becoming meaningful—"solitude weighs heavy," "silence is deafening," and "waste away in idleness."

I ordered myself to sleep.

In the morning, I woke up at the bell. I got up cheerfully, did everything as ordered. I made no violations.

I quickly lost count of the days. There was nothing to distinguish one from another. During my entire stay in the Big House, my "peace" was broken three times. Once two men came in.

"Any claims, any requests?"

"Questions, yes."

"We do not answer questions."

"Requests, then. I want to read and write."

"Writing is not permitted. You will read. That's all? "Yes."

A few days later, they handed me a thick book through the little window, *Malakov Hill*, by S. T. Grigoriev, Children's State Publishing House. A children's story about the defense of Sevastopol in the Crimean campaign.

I read it too fast. As with the sugar, I hadn't been told there was a monthly ration. And here I'd thought I'd be reading for days on end.

I reread the book. Then I started opening it at random and guessing as many words and sentences in advance as I could. Then I read it backward. That didn't improve it. I heartily detested this "true-to-life" historical novel. For lack of anything better to do, I started composing my own historical novel in my head in the same spirit of Socialist realism. That was a distraction.

"The well-designed rows of innumerable doors, a monolith of solidarity with their plainly marked numbers and chiseled peepholes, thanks to which not a single movement of the hardened criminal can escape; our heroic troops—the guards, that is—faithfully preserving ancient traditions even inside the walls of that astounding masterpiece of Russian architecture, the Peter and Paul Fortress; the soft, noiseless hallways, carpeted by the kilometer in an endless band covering corridors and stairways—the handiwork of our glorious toilers, who put into them all their boundless love for their mighty motherland, which stands firmly on . . . on carpeted hallways; and the exquisite, transparent, but strong wire grilles—all eliminate the possibility that any inveterate enemy of our beloved motherland might put an end to all these glorious traditions in one pitiful leap . . ."

That was how I amused myself. Sometimes I caught myself composing aloud. They didn't bring me any more books. No doubt *Malakov Hill* was thick enough to have exhausted my monthly ration.

Another time, a guard with an automatic came for me. Without a word, he led me down carpeted hallways past those innumerable, well-designed doors, up and down stairs lined with wire grilles. I went first with him just behind me. We occasionally saw people coming toward us, also in pairs. But according to a rule incomprehensible to me, on the command of the guard, either I or the person I passed would turn, facing the wall, into what seemed to be niches especially built for that purpose, and stand there until the oncoming pair had gone far enough that they could not be seen clearly. We arrived at a photographer's. He took three pictures of me. The full face had to be taken over because he didn't like my "grin," as he called it. "This is a serious business," he said, "there's nothing to grin at." We took the same route "home." I was delighted by the trip, completely delighted. So many new impressions! Enough for a whole new novel.

The third interruption was very entertaining. Following the same rules with about-faces into the niches, we arrived at a kind of laboratory. There, a man in a smock smeared all ten of my fingertips with something black and pressed them to a paper with special spaces reserved for each finger.

I got used to the pattern. I was no longer so sleepy by day. The idleness was the hardest to bear, but at least that first terror was gone. And I no longer felt so acutely sorry for myself. I could think, dream, even talk softly to myself or to Oleg—most often to Oleg. The important thing was not to break the strict regime; that meant the punishment cell.

Something evil was growing in me. Do I really love Oleg? If so, was I right not to tell him about myself? It wasn't because I was afraid of losing him that I avoided telling him, of course! That never occurred to me. But how much concern for Oleg was there in my silence and how much distrust? Or fear? And can love coexist with fear and distrust? If you have to maneuver through life, can your feelings be sincere? The something evil grew. It frightened me. I had always been kind, easily amused, compassionate. Now such blind hatred suddenly possessed me that I felt frightened. How could I live with it?

One night they came for me. They gave me almost a whole loaf of bread, two scrawny herrings, stiff as sticks of wood, white with their crust of salt. With difficulty, they shoved me into a small cage just inside the doors of a large, dark vehicle. I could hear men's voices from inside, through the closed doors. My cage didn't want to close, I had to fold my legs under me, but even so, there was barely enough room. I had spotted my bundle and suitcase in the passageway. It was very cold. What day was it today, I wondered? Could it be New Year's? Or maybe already January? I still don't know exactly how much time I spent in that building, but it must have been something like a month.

From the slow pace and two stops, I figured we had gone "through the locks," the two prison gates—this time, headed out. Where to?

## ON THE ROAD

"Stolypin Car," "Prison Car"—and what else did they call this jail on wheels? There was nothing remarkable about it from the outside. Inside, instead of the usual compartments, there were cages with three tiers of plank beds, and grilles with locks instead of doors. In addition, an armed guard paced the narrow corridor continuously.

Judging from the din on all sides, the car was crammed full. I, alone, traveled like a princess. There were only two of us in the entire cage: myself and a half-witted old biddy who sometimes stared at me with a steady, dull gaze, and at other times suddenly roared out underworld songs sprinkled with vulgar swear words in a hoarse, cracked, terrifying voice, with a smattering of Lithuanian or Latvian words. Whenever the guard came near our cage, my cellmate would jump out of her skin, calling: "Darling, darling, come on in, don't be scared, we won't eat you, we'll just have a little fun."

The guard would turn his head away. That always drove her to a frenzy, and she would rain down curses.

"Oh, you vulture in red shoulder tabs! Too young to shave and you turn your mug away from a woman like me. Oof, I'd like to strangle the viper with my own hands! I bet he's never even sniffed a woman yet, how would a shit like that get a woman? All the likes of him knows is how to guard prisoners; that, they're good at."

When he passed our cage again, he gave me a look of understanding. My cellmate exploded.

"Oh, my good people, hold me back or I'll burst laughing. He's staring at that fool girl again. Well, is she as much of a ninny as you, soldier? Look at her, rattling with fear, look at her, look—she's gnawing her hair off, getting ready to hang herself. Now go and complain, you good-for-nothing. Let them come get me right now to wash the floor so I can rest my eye on real men, not the likes of you, you milksop."

As a matter of fact, they used to come for her a couple of times a day after particularly stormy outbursts. They would twist her arms, drag her from the cage, and make her wash the floor of the corridor with ice-cold water. As she left, she shrieked at me, "Here I go for a walk again!"

We had been on the road three days. I was cold, and I knew what thirst is for the first time. Those two salted fishes and the bread they gave me in the Big House were supposed to last the journey, but they hadn't said how long it would be, so I'd gulped down the fish at one go. By now, I'd been miserable for three days, though more from thirst than hunger. Cry and beg as you like, there was nothing to drink all day. In the morning, they brought a pail of ice water. You drank as much as you could, and that was it for the day—ice water, on an empty stomach, and it made your teeth ache, too. I managed to drink a little bit. At night, I was freezing cold—and there came this ice water again. It was a very refined torture, but that wasn't all. "Relief" wasn't to be had for the asking either. As with water, it was available only in the morning and at night; during the day, you could burst. Because of the chill I had caught from the cold, this was harder on me than thirst. Yesterday someone in the next cell was soundly beaten; he, too, was unable to wait until evening. I had heard him whining, begging, howling, shouting that "the dogs would answer for it if he burst." Finally he used his own galosh in place of the latrine bucket, for which he was first brutally beaten, then made to wash the corridor of the entire car with ice water every two hours.

I was very cold. The wood bunks were bare, the walls of the car covered with ice. At least I had my own pillow and blanket, though the blanket was a very thin cotton flannel one, it's true. I sat wrapped in it all day, but the cold penetrated even so. From hunger and immobility, probably. My suitcase and bundle traveled with me. I even tried to knit, but my numbed fingers wouldn't obey. Still, I was glad to be on the road; it had to lead somewhere.

Unexpectedly, a guard spoke to me the first day. After looking around stealthily and seeing no one else from the convoy, he asked me:

"What are you in for, girl?"

"I don't know."

"You don't know. They all say the same thing. And you've probably committed enough sins for a lifetime. Now tell me the truth, what are you in for?"

"I tell you, I don't know. But I think it's for nothing."

"Don't lie. That doesn't happen."

He left. In about an hour, he came back and said: "The article you're arrested under is for escaping, girl. You'll get three years for that, anyway. You're so young, I'm sorry for you, you'll be done for in camp. I'm the same age as you, I'm nineteen, too. It's my first year in service, they sent me here with the red shoulder tabs right off. If you were free, you wouldn't even speak to me. Girls don't like the looks of us, with the red shoulder tabs. Who would, with our kind of work? Why, when they let you free and you go back to Leningrad, you won't even speak to me if we meet!"

The boy poured his heart out at length, thanks to the guards' being away, probably getting drunk. My cellmate was sitting, dozing, having yelled herself out. My heart shrank when he said "three years, anyway."

"How do you know I'm here for 'escaping'? And that they give three years for that?"

"I opened up your record. We're allowed to in special cases. And you're a special case, all the chaps are interested in it. We don't escort the likes of you every day. And how come you don't look Jewish? You'll get three years if you're lucky. They can give more. Less than three, never."

How could that be? Escape? Three years in prison? But what about my life, my love, my happiness? Three years without sun, without books? And why say I *escaped*? I didn't run away from anyplace, I left completely legally, so why was it called escaping now? I'd simply made up my mind one day after finishing seventh grade and said to Mama, "That's it, Mama, let me go or I'll hang myself. I can't live here anymore. I don't want to croak here. Let me go peacefully."

Mama knew it was best to let me go peacefully. And now they called it an *escape*. It wasn't a very jolly picture, but I'd learned by then that you can't let yourself go. Shed one little tear for yourself and you'll see, you'll be streaming tears, you'll be racked by feelings of injury, of despair, you won't want to live. Later I learned the boy was right about my being arrested under the article for *escape*. But it was put in out of humanitarian considerations, I was told—could that be thanks to the handsome young man in Leningrad?—so I would be considered under investigation and would be sent on to my destination quicker.

They removed my crazy cellmate the third night, and the following day we arrived somewhere. Our car was switched about, uncoupled, and left standing. I heard voices. Then the men were taken out; that took a long time. Afterward, they took me out with my bundle and suitcase. There stood a kind of van—a "Black Bertha," "Black Maria," "Black Raven"—a gloomy-looking black vehicle from which came cursing, gutter language, howling, and singing. They drove the men inside. I was again put in a little pen next to the door, but this time I was so numb I couldn't fold my legs under. The guard left my door half ajar to avoid cutting them off, and we set out.

I could see a little through the tiny window in the back door of the van. As I recognized the places we drove through, my heart contracted in pain. We were near Oleg's house. Half a year ago, he had met me at this very station. It's here we took a bus, then were forced to spend the night because we just missed our connection. How happy we were then. We listened to the nightingales . . . a woman gave up her own bed for us . . . and I felt embarrassed in front of her the next morning as if she knew we weren't man and wife.


The transit prison was old and wooden. I tumbled out of the van, my legs rigid in my boots; I could no longer feel them. While the guards checked and recounted endlessly, they sat me down on my bundle, where I stayed, rubbing my legs. Several groups of prisoners arrived. The women were taken to the "Sanitary Facility"—the bathhouse, that is. That was a bath to end all baths. There was a minuscule dressing room with a luxuriant layer of frost over the walls and a thin carpet of ice on the floor. Naked, skeletal, shivering women turned over their clothing (which was sent to be deloused) and went into the so-called bath. At the entrance, each was counted and given a smidgen of black soap the size of a schoolboy's eraser. From a pipe in the ceiling dripped a little barely warm water. It was almost as cold as in the dressing room. When we asked to have the water turned on, they said there was no pressure; it was awfully cold and awkward trying to catch a few drops. We were ordered to wash our hair, too. I barely managed to cope with my braids at home; here, my head came out looking like a hunk of felt, though I didn't catch cold from the bath. All the same, I began doggedly chewing off my braids. The rugged hairstyle I created later provoked a lot of amusement among my cellmates.

Women were sitting, lying, and walking about in the cell to which they took me after the so-called bath. A continuous row of two-story plank beds lined three walls; a latrine bucket stood by the door, and just under the ceiling was a tiny, frost-coated window. I stood, dumbstruck, at the door.

"Why are you standing there like a stump? Haven't you seen people before?" came a pleasant woman's voice from somewhere above.

"Come make yourself at home, this isn't a theater."

"Girls, she's deaf and dumb. Or maybe she had a stroke?"

The woman making fun of me was young and attractive. She cleared a space beside her on the second story of bunks and invited me into her "parlor" with a welcoming gesture.

Her name was Zhenya. I thawed out beside her. They gave me hot tea with sugar, and Zhenya buttered a thick piece of bread for me. I loved the whole world and looked at Zhenya with adoration.

She turned out to be a good teacher. She had a solid stretch: seven years behind her, eight to go—"and then they'll probably add some anyway," said Zhenya. She was only twenty-six. They had just taken her from a camp in Kazakhstan to Leningrad to testify on some case.

And where they were taking her now, God knows. Perhaps Kazakhstan, perhaps Kolyma—it didn't matter, she spat on all of it. One way or another, her life was hopeless.

I believed every word Zhenya said. She talked on and on. Every story was of a maimed life, of lost years, of sorrow, and the stories seemed without end. The most terrible part was that just a month or two earlier, I would never have believed what she said. I might not even have listened. It would have seemed preposterous, monstrous, a pack of lies. How could such things happen? Where was justice? I brushed away that thought, telling myself to be honest: "You knew there wasn't any justice. It was simply more convenient not to think about it. Take your own father, why was he in prison for ten years?" It seems that to believe these things, you have to go through them yourself. And more important, to understand. Once you've understood, like Zhenya, you can't keep still.

Zhenya talked and talked. About her parents, about friends, about strangers. She had been in prison with so many people. I lay beside her on the bunk and whispered, horrified, "Zhenechka, how can such things happen? How can innocent people—completely innocent, if anything too honest—be made to suffer and die like that? Why there's no reason for it, absolutely no reason. How can it be? What's going to happen?"

"It's a tyranny, a terrible tyranny. Somebody finds it convenient and doesn't hesitate to make use of it. If he hesitated, he'd go under himself. Nobody knows what would happen if the machine stopped, so everyone just looks out for his own skin. And keeps still. Waiting. Thinking maybe it'll pass."

"When did you first catch on?"

"I wised up in camp. I was a fool at first, like you."

"What's going to happen? I want so much to live."

"That's the terrible thing, there's no end in sight. But don't give up. Maybe they'll still let you go. I'm obviously doomed to go knocking about camps, yet even I have a little hope left."

The most tragic part of Zhenya's story, in my eyes, concerned the birth of her child. She was pregnant when arrested, and gave birth to a daughter in prison two months later. She saw her child for only a few minutes after it was born, and had known nothing about it since. Her husband was arrested a few days before she was, both accused of underground activities for a foreign power. Zhenya had a difficult pregnancy. That, she explained, is why she couldn't hold out long; after a few days, she signed all the accusations against her. They gave her fifteen years. Her husband wasn't like that, no—he wasn't one to sign a lot of nonsense. For all I know he was shot long ago. Now, in seven years in prison, Zhenya had been in Kazakhstan, in Siberia, in the far north, and had seen more prisoner convoys and transit prisons than she could count. This one was the best kind because it was in a settlement instead of a big town.

"There's no end in sight," Zhenya said, and that's why she "walked under the bunks." There was a fairly large hole in the wall under the lower bunks that was painstakingly hidden from the administration; you could reach right through to the men's cell next door. To judge from the noise, the cell next door was huge. Only young women "walked under the bunks," and in strictly observed order. What happened there, I don't know. It was awkward to ask, but when the woman whose turn it was reappeared, even those who had seen everything, like Zhenya, looked away. And a silence fell.

One night it was Zhenya's turn. I fell asleep after she left, but was awakened by her crying. The bunk was shaking with suppressed sobs. I touched her shoulder.

She brushed my hand away, and when I asked what had happened, she suddenly went into hysterics. She shouted, rolled about the bunk, tore her clothing and hair, made contortions, and swore fearfully. Curses rained. All the women gathered around us; the old ones shook their heads. They tried to quiet Zhenya—they feared being sent to the punishment cell for making noise at night.

Little by little, Zhenya became calmer, but between sobbing and nose blowing, you could hear the words, "Swine, what swine!" To whom she referred, I don't know—the men in the next cell or those responsible for all of this—but I comforted her as best I could. Strangely enough, despite the gap in our ages, despite Zhenya's experience and the many marked differences between us, she listened attentively to what I said and wearily nodded her head. I was inspired. Where did the words come from? Thoughts I'd never had before flowed spontaneously. In a passionate whisper, I begged her not to ruin her health; her daughter might yet need her, perhaps her husband, too. I told her one must not lose one's pride (there she smiled crookedly), that the end to this nightmare would come. It couldn't go on like this forever—Zhenya should remember examples from history. One had to believe that. If you lost faith, it was the end of everything.

One must be courageous, never let oneself go. She was young, beautiful; even after another eight years, she would still have a life ahead, so why torture herself so? One could not "walk under the bunks" and then damn the whole world.

"Stupid, you're still a child, but thank you. Go to sleep now."

The days dragged on monotonously. In the mornings, there was a diversion in the corridor. On the way to the washroom, the women used to rush, squealing, to the little window in the door to the men's cell and shout something. The guards scolded them, even laid hands on them, but they didn't care. They were driven with difficulty into the washroom. There, in the most unexpected places, they'd find notes and leave others behind, and write mysterious words and symbols on the facebowl in thin lines of toothpaste. On the way back, there was the same race to the men's cell, and then came a mug of warm water with a piece of bread, the latrine bucket detail, and then the whole rest of the day—continuous inactivity. For dinner there was a bowl of disgusting, nauseating soup (known as "wishwash" here), and, in the evening, a mug of tea. I was terribly hungry, particularly in the evenings, but that was my own fault for eating my entire ration of bread in the morning.

Ten days went by like that. One morning, Zhenya and I were called out for transfer. How glad I was not to be separated from her yet.

We waited a long time. They counted us, recounted us, checked, took one away, brought out another. First there was no van, then not enough guards. There were men, too, kept separate from us, but in the same guarded area. I concluded I'd worried about Zhenya's morals in vain. She started behaving unnaturally, rolled her eyes, made peculiar gestures, and did everything she could to attract attention, while the men neighed coarse laughs like stallions. I was extremely embarrassed.

A tall, good-looking boy, strangely at odds with the crowd of ragamuffins around him, gave me a very pleasant smile from a distance. He had on white felt boots, a luxurious fur hat, and a very handsome winter overcoat. When they took us away, he smiled at me once more and waved his hand.

Another long, cold trip brought us to the station. The "Stolypin" was locked and the cold had become fierce. Suddenly, a young fellow in the crowd of ragged men fell down on the dirty ice, clutching and beating himself.

His eyes rolled and he foamed at the mouth. He didn't even have a real coat, just the remnants of a jacket. He wheezed, contorted himself, beat his head on the ice. His buddies restrained him. The guard came running. The key was found. When they got the car open, the first one to jump in was the man who had "a fit", who earned himself a kick in the behind from the guard. I thought it was epilepsy.

On the road once again. We traveled for a whole week, longer than the first time, but we spent most of it on sidings. The car was crowded. There were obviously other prisons in the town, for there were more than ten people in our compartment. That's what made it warm. Zhenya was next to me. Again, we were given a wooden stick of herring for the trip, but I had an experienced teacher with me. Zhenya exchanged my salt fish for a good-sized piece of bread, and I didn't get as thirsty this time.

This time, the guards never spoke, they just shouted orders. The women weren't beaten, but in the next compartment, where the men were, there were shouts announcing a search every few hours, and blows rained right and left among groans and foul language.

Zhenya and I talked for hours about many things. I found it strange to speak for the first time in my life about things I had always delicately avoided—about prisons, executions, idiotic accusations of unimaginable crimes; about life in general, with nothing held back. But sometimes I bored Zhenya, and she would abruptly change into a fury. She would use foul language and, spoiling for a fight, insult some woman and come to blows with her over a trifle. Only the threats of the guard would bring her back to reason. When she turned to me, she'd say appeasingly, with a crooked smile, though still shaking with emotion, "I had to get it off my chest. You're such a greenhorn, so naïve, my heart turns over just looking at you. Seven years ago, I was exactly like you. Pure, kind. And now I'm garbage like the rest. God grant you get out of here quickly. And don't look at me so pityingly. It's anger over my ruined life that makes me pounce on these fools. They're all swine. They are common criminals, you see. They couldn't find room for them so they put them in with us political prisoners. If it were the other way around, if there were more of them, the bitches would be lording it over us because we're the enemy even to these pigs. They'd have stripped you to the skin by now, and there you sit, thank God, still decked out like a princess. Even your stockings aren't very torn yet. If you stay in prison, you'd do better to exchange your clothes for something warmer, but I think they'll let you go. They'll transport you, maybe let you sit in prison a while as a warning, but they'll let you go."

Prison again, another transit prison. This time a modern one, brick. And—shame. Shame to make your head swim, to make you want to die on the spot. A medical inspection, it was called. Administered by one so-called nurse (female) and two young men who didn't even bother to put on smocks. The signs in the room where the women undressed on one side and the men on the other explained it was an "inspection for antisocial diseases." It was a very humiliating procedure, and as long as I'm allowed to go on living in this accursed world, I won't forget it.

I spent about two weeks in that prison. The cell was crammed with about thirty people, all political prisoners—wives of big Party men, actresses, many foreigners. A tall, plump, authoritative woman, a Jewess, the recognized leader in the cell, had been in prison almost twelve years. She and her husband were arrested a few days before the war for spying for the Germans. Her husband was shot; she got twenty-five years. There were wives of traitors, even the wife of a traitor general, a former ballerina. Still she walked around the cell with her legs turned out a bit and her face was like a dried-up cameo. It was hardest on the foreigners, who had no common tongue and were obviously used to living better before. It wasn't that they looked spoiled, but they all looked as though they had never imagined anything of this sort, and their expressions asked: "Why? What for? How can it be?"

There was a novel diversion, too. Two young German women, arrested for contact with West Berlin (they both had boyfriends there), left each night to wash the guards' laundry. In the mornings, they came back to the cell with bread, cigarettes, and sometimes candy and margarine. They used to talk to one another in German, saying, "How? With how many?" and giving details. I was on the next bunk and never got up the courage to tell them I understood their chatter; I should have done it at the beginning. How the cell laughed when one old woman suddenly declared, "So why always the same girls, the same girls?" and said she'd go do laundry, too, by heaven. The younger women whooped with laughter, the older ones chuckled, and when the truth about this nightly laundry got through to the old grandmother, she spat in exasperation and said, looking angrily at the Germans, "Phoo, a Fritz is a Fritz is a Fritz."

Once again I was lucky; I was assigned to the same convoy as Zhenya. Again there were cold, hunger, thirst, beatings in the next cell, ferocious swearing, nightly searches. I was faint from constant hunger, my head was spinning, I had trouble walking. Zhenya said I was weakening before her eyes, that a skeleton was fatter and better looking. By that time I had almost gnawed my braids away; Zhenya was probably right; it wasn't the kind of place where beauty thrives.

We were escorted on foot to the next transit prison
by a convoy with guard dogs. It was my introduction
to this splendid kind of escort. The few women went
first, followed by a column of ragamuffins—the men,
carrying knapsacks, wooden boxes, and suitcases. Sur-
rounding this mob were guards with automatics and
quiet-paced, handsome Alsatians.

This was my third transit prison. I was even becoming
used to them and to the constant cold, the gnawing
hunger, and circumstances in general. It was interesting.
I thought about myself less. I often mourned for Oleg,
but somehow not for "us"; rather, I forced myself to
picture, sadly, his future life without me. I felt no sorrow
over losing "a good husband," no; I only regretted he
would never know the truth about anything as I knew
it. Not that I would want him to go through *that*; but
I knew now that if we met, soon or after many years,
there would be the same wall between us again, which,
for Oleg's happiness, I would be careful not to destroy.
Yet now that I had come to understand, I probably would
no longer be able to live behind a wall. That made me
very sad, as if it were not life that had betrayed me,
but I who had betrayed Oleg.

Parting with Zhenya was sad. I was called out for
a convoy and she remained behind. There was no time
for tears. At the shout, "Out the door!" there was no
dallying. I grabbed my things and ran. Zhenya gave me
the postal number of her last camp and asked me to
write her and send paper and envelopes if I was set free.
We choked back a sob and kissed each other.

The wheels ground once again. My cage was very
crowded. In fact, the whole car was filled to overflowing.
The men didn't even have room to sit. They were cursing
and brawling. The women were clawing and biting each
other, too; the guards kept separating them. One spiteful

girl cursed me, threatening to "knock off the bourgeois student" because my suitcase and bundle took up too much space in the compartment. How did she spot me so accurately? It wasn't written on my forehead that I was a student, was it? I didn't say a word to anyone. They weren't there to make friends and talk, they were baring their teeth at each other because they had no room. There were, furthermore, only a few political prisoners among all the criminals. The third day, they took the criminals out, leaving only two of us in the cage, a gentle, quiet woman and myself. Immediately the cold struck. But before this the frenzied, sweaty bodies had rendered the atmosphere unbreathable and caused water to run down the walls. I thought my damp clothes would freeze to my body.

My cellmate was a very fine woman. She was imprisoned "for religion," she said. She shook her head sadly on hearing how old I was, saying she would pray that still another innocent soul would not be lost. We huddled together under my thin cotton flannel blanket and dreamed of hot tea.

I spent four days at the next transit prison "living" right next to the latrine bucket, afraid to move. There were five terrorists and about forty women in the cell, all terrified. I've never seen such bestiality in my life. In comparison with these furies, the poor souls who scrapped in the train because they were overcrowded seemed like lambs. My gentle old lady religious prisoner tried to appeal to the conscience of these shrews.

"Calm yourselves, girls, when our life is so hard, why make it worse?"

"And who are you to tell me what to do?" one handsome girl belonging to the "terrorists" said, going up to her.

"I'm not telling you what to do. I suffer for you, my

daughter. Why do you swear like that? It's shameful to hear. And it's a sin to keep innocent people in fear. No one's done you any harm, you're angry for nothing, you're just destroying your own soul with your anger. You don't know how much easier things are for good people. Anger blinds people, chokes them so they can't understand even simple words. Try it, my girl, and tell your comrades."

"What do you mean, try it? I've tried everything, by all the principles of dialectical materialism. Why, I was positively an angel, but they stamped on the innocent little flower without looking," the beauty said, articulating each syllable maliciously. I almost jumped at the sharply enunciated "dialectical materialism" and the nasal twang of "innocent little flower."

"You must suffer in patience, my girl, you mustn't bear malice, it's too hard to live with."

"What do you mean, suffer in patience? I've suffered enough. I've suffered things you've never dreamed of, Old Lady Christian. Every swine lorded it over me to his heart's content until I lost my innocence—but not everybody will try to take advantage of somebody who hits back. You're a fool, Grandma. It's easier to live my way, not yours. And don't pester me about sin, I don't believe in sin anymore and I'll push your ugly mug in."

"Moralist, hypocrite! Give it to her Lenka, what's she preaching here for? We are more educated than you, but we don't give a shit, we get by as best we can. There's no point going on about it. Don't tell us what to do, Grandma. I'll smash your face in—that'll stop you poisoning the hearts of innocent young girls."

Lenka clipped the old woman round the ear—not very hard, but noisily and arrogantly. The old woman's tears flowed. Everyone was silent. Lenka tossed her cigarette into the latrine bucket, met my look, turned back to the old woman once more, and crawled onto her bunk with her comrades. They laughed scornfully, slapped Lenka on the shoulder, gave her another cigarette.

I was afraid to look in her direction. I felt she was not in control of herself, yet I was very curious about her. Those five intrepid girls did not look like criminals —how had they come to live like that? I didn't dare approach them or even glance in their direction.

That night I woke up when my head slid off my bundle, which served me as a pillow. I saw one of the "terrorists" from the "powerful five" leaning over me and cautiously pulling my only scarf out of my bundle, right from under my head. I rose up in astonishment. Making a gesture of cutting her throat with one hand, she rolled her eyes, pulled the scarf all the way out with the other hand, and calmly climbed back into her bunk on the second level. The following day, paying no attention to me, she appeared wearing my scarf. I just watched and wondered.

SURPRISE

Even in places like that, there are surprises. Pleasant ones. Until then I had watched, listened, groveled, and gone through such terror that I at first didn't understand what was up when a soldier from the convoy looked stealthily around and suddenly began unlocking my cage for no apparent reason. Then—plop!—a package fell on my knees.

A miracle! Once again, for the second day, I was alone in the compartment. I sat motionless. It seemed to me my blood was barely flowing through my veins. I had had no strength since morning. I didn't even feel very thirsty, and I'd gotten so used to being hungry that it no longer tormented me. The bad part was that my strength was running out and I was very depressed. It

was better being with crazy people, with thieves, just
to be with human beings.

I had been on the road over a month. We stopped
in Novosibirsk, where I wasn't kept long in the prison.
If they were taking me to the place of my former exile,
I wouldn't have much longer to wait—one more stop,
Krasnoyarsk, after which I'd be in the town where Mother
lived. The thought made me happy and frightened. What
if they didn't let me go?

The wheels ground monotonously, the guard paced
the narrow corridor with measured steps. He would walk
up to my cage, the last in the car, and back, and so
on all day. Then a new guard came on who made me
feel uneasy. The new one didn't walk monotonously;
he walked busily, cautiously, and kept going up to my
cage and glancing in in a suspicious way. I was afraid
he might have evil intentions. You could shout all you
liked here, but no one would come to your rescue.

But then he glanced around stealthily and threw me
the package, and the stub of a pencil dropped out on
my lap as I turned it over—well, it was a miracle, that's
all. There was candy in the package. I was moved beyond
belief. *Candy!* And a real pencil. Ten pieces of candy,
wonderful candy, chocolate—or maybe it was soybean.
I ate them all then and there. They were wrapped in
a note with a signature—Vladimir Voznesensky. I had
no idea who he was, but that was unimportant, he was
a fine fellow. What a feast he had given me. I picked
up the note.

Who are you, Vladimir, with such a heavenly name?*
And how did you find out my name? And how did you
manage to seek me out here and send me such a royal
gift? How important you must be to have a pencil! Thank
you, my darling, with a heart of gold. How good it is

---

*Vosnesensky is derived from *vosneseniye,* meaning "ascension."

to be alive. Of course, I'll answer all your questions and follow all your advice:

1. Don't be discouraged . . . But I'm not discouraged.

2. Don't be afraid of anything . . . But what can I do if it's frightening?

3. Give me an address right away where you can possibly be after this journey . . . All right, we'll think of something.

The pencil was a centimeter and a half long, but even that was a treasure. On the back of his note, I scribbled: "If you're not an angel, who are you? I never ate anything more delicious in my life. Thank you. I have no address, I'm on my way to prison. I'm sending Mama's address, she'll know where I am. Thank you, thank you. Life is better now, life is happier!"

I'd barely finished writing when the cage door opened and the guard whispered, "Give it here!" I gave him the note. He demanded the pencil, too (I was just considering how to hide it), then grunted, "Don't expect an answer, I don't want to be taking your place on account of your intrigues."

"Citizen chief, who sent this?" I asked, emboldened at last.

"What do you mean, who? As if you didn't know. Why, your handsome correspondent, it's the second day he's given me no peace, it's always, 'Find out her name, find out her name.' And you've got a tricky name, I had to copy it down."

But he saw from my face I really didn't know who my benefactor was.

"He's tall, white felt boots, still wears a shaggy cap, and is all sleek still, not shabby. Well?"

Of course I recognized him. He had waved good-bye to me. As a matter of fact, he was the only man I'd seen on the whole trip who wasn't in rags. Yet he was with a criminal transport. What did you do, Vladimir? Kill, rob, rape? People aren't sent away as criminals for nothing. But does it matter to me? How much warmth, how much kindness you showed me! Everything looked better now, I even felt stronger.

I thought of him all day and pictured how when they let me go, I'd find out his address and send him the most delicious package so he, too, would have a holiday out of human kindness.

### CLOSE TO HOME

The train barely crept along. Our car stood on the rails somewhere for a long time, then was coupled to an engine and rocked back and forth. We obviously hadn't been hitched to a fast train. If they left me on the train longer than twenty-four hours, it would mean we'd gone past Krasnoyarsk, meaning I wouldn't see the house where I grew up, meaning—prison. I remembered, five and a half years ago, lying on dusty mattresses on the baggage shelf from Kansk station to Krasnoyarsk and dying with fear that the conductor would discover me traveling without a ticket. It took eight hours then.

I was so agitated now, I felt we'd been traveling all eternity, though the train stood still most of the time. One day went by. I saw night through the window. I was alone in the compartment, but I knew the men's section was crammed full. I could hear them changing the watch; those standing lay down and those sleeping stood up. Again there wasn't room enough for all of them to sit. They were beaten constantly, too. There was swearing, fighting, and that very night there had already been two searches. I heard it all through a fog, and was so groggy and weak all over that I saw circles before my eyes.

Another stop. Near our car, I heard bustling, wheezing, muffled voices. Then, suddenly, a distinct roar. I raised myself a little. "Aha! Dogs!" That meant there were convoy guards next to the car, which meant they were taking people off now, which meant there was a transit prison here. It'd be nice to know what town it was. "If only I'm taken off, too!" I should knock and ask. Why am I sitting here? But I'd grown so tired in the last few days that I was content when I found a little space right next to the latrine bucket, where I could lie all day. Even if the bedbugs pestered me and the air was foul and close, there were human beings around, it was warm, and there was warm tea twice a day.

I heard doors bang, a bustling, and at last: "Get ready!"

"Fine!" There was nothing to get ready, nothing to put away, nothing but bare bunks.

I was always taken out either first or last because, as they explained, "a woman isn't allowed with men, they might do all kinds of things."

There was already a crowd of ragged men beside the car, about forty of them, and guards with dogs. How cold it was! Forty below, for sure. Must be February. I wonder what day?

"Form ranks! The female in front! The men, four in a row! Get moving, no talking."

The female—that was me. I was used to it. Everyone moved fast. In cold like that, you don't stand around, especially with the dogs standing by.

This time, too, they had unloaded us on a siding—obviously so the prisoners wouldn't know where they were being taken, and also so people coming to the station wouldn't see how many there were.

Our column marched in the black of the frozen night. The town was dark. It was a procession of gnomes! A guard with a dog went in front; behind him, myself; on either side, another guard with a dog; behind, by fours, the men; around them, still more guards with automatics and dogs. Each guard had a lantern, a warm fur jacket, a fur cap, felt boots, and mittens. In a few minutes, I could no longer feel my feet; my thin boots seemed frozen to my heels. My poor overcoat, with its "rippling back," was obviously not designed for Siberian cold. On my head was a silk kerchief. Exhausted, hungry, stumbling, I was too weak to drag my suitcase and bundle. I tottered. The dog glanced at me, but the guard evidently understood I was unable to go on. He ordered the men to take my bundle and suitcase. They swore, but took them. I walked more easily.

We walked a considerable distance. I tried to make out the names of the streets, but could see no more than a few steps ahead in the cold and dark. All the same, I felt a growing agitation, my heart beat fast. Of course! It was the same street I'd gone down with Mama on a similar freezing, dark night a few years ago, dying with fear as we ran to the station to meet my cousin on his way back from the Far East. Oh Lord! I remembered that the way to the local prison led past the house where we lived. I'd seen columns of prisoners on our street many times, but it had never occurred to me I might someday be one of them. "It's strange it never occurred to me!" I thought.

Where does a human being find his strength? I had just been staggering, afraid of falling, and now wings had sprouted. I even merited a glance from the Alsatian's handsome, intelligent eyes—was this woman getting ready to run off now? My thoughts brightened, too. "How handsome the dogs are, what intelligent faces, they don't look frightening, though they can bite for sure."

We were going right to our street. Just two more turns and there, second from the corner, was the house where Mama lived. Mama's asleep, dreaming, unaware her darling is marching in close ranks right past her. It's a good thing she can't see me, or she'd surely collapse.

One thought wilder than the next raced through my

mind. Knock on the window! Leap over the fence and hide in the shed! (Would it be closed? Impossible.) Shout out loud—but the shutters are closed, she wouldn't hear me. I had to do something to let her know, otherwise maybe we'd never see each other again!

Along with the dogs, the guard began to sense something was wrong and started watching me. This was the street. I saw my house, just a few steps away. Lord! What could I do? I thought I would faint. Then suddenly, right in front of the house, came the order: "Halt!" Everyone stopped. I was afraid to believe it. Were they letting me go home?

No, it wasn't for that.

"Men—relieve yourselves. Woman, two steps forward, don't turn around."

So be it, this wasn't the first time. Bitterly I reflected that no one would bother to think of me even once and say, "Men, don't look around." To say something, to ask, embarrassed me; they'd laugh. That must be why I had a pain in my loins. Suddenly colic seized me so badly my eyesight grew dim.

"Citizen chief! Citizen chief!" I called out over the drizzle behind my back. "Let me go in that house for a minute, my mother lives there. Or let me just knock at the window."

"You'll be knocking on the walls of the punishment cell!" the citizen chief barked, though not unkindly.

What a fool I was to appeal to him—but I hadn't thought rationally, I was just desperate. They were leading me away, and Mama would never know how close I had been.

We walked on.

Though they did not let me in my house, the citizen chief was right about the punishment cell. Two hours later I found myself there.

## THE PUNISHMENT CELL

When we arrived it was probably four or five in the morning. Oh, what a row there was. The convoy guard and the man on duty swore at each other over me. The prison was a criminal one, the convoy arriving was criminal, and there was I, out of the blue, a political prisoner. There was no place to put me. Some fun! There was no cell for political prisoners in the prison, and the rules forbade putting me with criminals—I might corrupt them, God forbid. I heard the man on duty hiss at the convoy leader:

"Have you grown stupid or what? Didn't you see who you were taking? She's not ours, so we shouldn't touch her."

"Yes, but there were none of them there, so what was to be done with her? She was put off the train, they weren't taking her farther."

"That's not your problem. She's theirs—let them pick her up. And suppose she was sent on, they'd manage without you. What am I supposed to do with her now? Put her at my desk? I don't have places to put their people. You took her, you take her."

"Come on, where'm I to take her? It's night, there's nobody there."

"Don't talk nonsense, they work all night, and furthermore there's always someone on duty."

Finally, they found a solution. Their punishment cell was empty. They didn't need such a fearful place for "bluebloods" like robbers and murderers.

The heavy metal door opened. Bundle and suitcase in hand, I stepped into darkness. It was pitch-black, cold, icy, damp, and smelled like a cellar. There was slush underfoot, something sticky and slippery. I was tired of holding my suitcase and bundle, but how could I put them down in that muck? Gingerly, I took a few steps forward and leaned the bundle against the slippery, icy wall. There I dropped my load. I reached out and leaned against the slimy walls. It was a crypt.

Something dripped steadily from the ceiling. Or maybe it was the silence beating, maybe I was going out of my mind? I remembered the Chinese torture in which they keep water dripping steadily on a prisoner's head until he goes crazy from what seems like thundering drops. I became frightened. What if I went mad with fear? Started shouting in my insanity with no one to hear? Or fainted in that mud? I struggled to calm myself. I hadn't been put in the punishment cell forever. Sooner or later they'd come to feed me, so they'd find me even if I fainted. And perhaps it would soon be over.

Suddenly something squeaked. Rats! I jumped. I had the feeling they wouldn't reach my neck as quickly if I remained standing. Skeletons picked clean flashed before my eyes; the darkness of the cell was transformed by flashing, kaleidoscopic skulls and crossbones, cat-sized rats, a whole attack force of them, white and fat, able to take castles by storm. The slop underfoot spread and rose. It was already up to my knees, soon I'd choke. Rats can swim on the surface of mud; it makes it even easier for them to get to your throat. I was terrified. I had no more judicious arguments, no hope in sight, yet I clutched at something . . . Ah, yes, who painted "The Princess Tarakanova"? It began with *F* or *T*. There were rats and water in the picture, too, I think. It wasn't exactly the same; the princess was dying. But maybe they saved her? That's always the way. What a dummy—how come you don't know whether they saved her or not? They didn't save her, and they won't save you . . .

I let out a wild, terrible shriek. I could still hear the beginning of the cry as I slithered and groped my way to the door and began beating on it. Again I heard myself shriek when the key grated in the lock, and my first clear thought was, "They beat you for doing this." Lord, let them, so long as I have people around instead of rats and that terrifying darkness.

The same night guard opened the door. He looked at me a moment. He wasn't going to beat me, not even swear at me. Quietly, he said, "Well, what are you knocking for, girl? Disturbing good people's sleep?"

I'd have been so happy to sit under his desk if only it were allowed. It was so frightening to think he would go away now. My teeth chattered, my whole body shook.

"I'm frightened, there are rats here, it's so dark, I'm so afraid. I'm terrified. Please don't lock me in."

"It's a punishment cell, not a sanatorium on the Black Sea. But there aren't any rats, and if there were, they wouldn't touch you. They're scared of people. I've no place to put you, girl. I know myself it's frightening. But I can't put you in the general cell. Be patient. In the morning, I'll call up the people responsible and tell them to send a horse. I don't think you'd make it on foot. Don't be afraid; I'm sitting close by, you just don't hear me. And I'm forbidden to talk to prisoners. As it is, I'm breaking the rules . . ."

The door closed again, but I wasn't a bit frightened. Really, wasn't it shameful to be such a coward? How do I think up these horrors? Furthermore, the artist's name was Flavitsky, how could I forget? Still, it all happened—just a few minutes back, it all happened not to just anybody—to me. So that's how people go out of their minds. I'd never have been able to smile so calmly at my foolish fears if the guard hadn't opened the door. Oh, you kind man, you saved me. Thank you! You comforted me, even promised to ask for a horse. There are still good people in the world. Why, he even broke the rules talking to me. Thank you, Uncle.

Teetering through the mud, I reached my corner, sat

down, and sank into thought. That's the way man is.
Save him from death or insanity—he's glad, and oh! so
grateful. But once the danger's past, the mean thoughts
sneak up:

The scoundrels, how am I to blame for their not having
a place to put political prisoners? And what kind of political malefactor am I anyway? How would I corrupt these
sheeplike criminals? With my ideology? I wouldn't
breathe it to a soul. Who talks about ideologies, attitudes,
and international relations anyway? And why doesn't
anyone know what's going on? Take my friend Lyalya,
for example. She'll die never knowing how many innocent people are suffering. Her father has a portrait of
Stalin hanging in his study, and the bookcases along
the walls in her house overwhelm you with thick tomes
by our revolutionary leaders. I wonder what she'll say
when she hears about me. And what about Oleg? Was
he frightened? They'll put him down as having contact
with an enemy of the people, and his whole career will'
be ruined. It won't help that we weren't married. He's
probably afraid to write—no, he's not like that. Oleg is
very honest. There are probably lots of honest people,
but they have to keep quiet to avoid getting killed or
going out of their minds. Take the guard, even. What
a fine man he is! Just think, I'm not frightened at all
now. Bah, why rats, why white ones, and why "Princess
Tarakanova"? And why would rats have to get to your
throat, you idiot? They're perfectly capable of starting
with your feet. Something really is squeaking, but it
sounds more like mice. And I'm not afraid of anything.
In the morning, they'll send a horse for me. All I'd like
to know is where they'll take me and if they'll let me
go, and if not, whether I can let Mama know. All in
all, my thoughts are mixed up. How good it was with
Oleg, how warm and cozy. I'd like some hot tea, it

wouldn't even have to be sweet, and it doesn't matter
if I lean on the wall, my coat is already dirty anyway.
It even has holes here and there and no buttons left.
It'll be too bad if they don't let me go.

I came to in the corridor. Two men were holding me
under the arms, trying to put me on my feet, but I kept
falling. It was terribly embarrassing. They dragged me
to a chair. I could hear everything clearly and understand,
but I couldn't see anything, and the worst part was that
I had no feeling in my legs. One of the two men stood
beside my chair, holding me up with his side while checking something the guard on duty had in his hands. Papers
rustled.

I felt myself with my hands. My coat was slimy and
wet, meaning I'd been lying on the floor. Not for very
long, apparently, only a few hours, because the guard
had said he'd call "them" in the morning to send a horse.

Little by little I could see light. I began breathing more
evenly and shrank away from the stranger's side. "I can
sit by myself." I could even wiggle my foot. Everything
was in order. At the table stood a young man with papers
in his hand—the courier from the other place, the one
that had failed to send anyone to the station for me the
night before. He had an attentive and sympathetic look,
friendly even.

"Shall we go on foot or be carried?" he said ironically.
He was the first to address me politely.

"On foot."

"Fine, fine."

I fell down right there by the chair, unable to stand
on my feet; it was as though they weren't there. The
young man swept me into his arms, told the guard to
bring my things, and carried me into the street. The sun
was shining! The snow sparkled! At the entrance stood

a horse, hitched to a two-seated sleigh. He set me down like a package, took up the reins, and oh Lord, there were jingling bells on the horse's neck. Like in a movie!

## WELCOME!

I knew where we were going. I used to walk past that building twice a day on the way to school. And twice a month Mama went there to register. Sometimes she took me along, leaving me to wait on the street in case something happened to her. It amused me to remember Mama pulling tufts of wool out of her thread-bare sweater, putting on her "chic" skirt of sackcloth, and wiping off all traces of lipstick. She thought she had to make them think she lived badly, that the more downtrodden she looked, the less risk she ran of being sent to a camp or to the far north. She never went near this building when she walked somewhere—God forbid, she always crossed to the other side of the street. We were headed for the NKVD, and by the same route of the night before. Without hope, but figuring I had nothing to lose, I asked:

"Citizen chief, couldn't we stop a moment in that house over there?"

"What for?"

"My mother lives there, she doesn't know I'm here."

He thought a moment. My heart pounded.

He turned the horse toward the house. So that was that! But the shutters were closed as they had been last night, meaning Mama was at work. I ventured:

"Since you're so kind, citizen chief, perhaps we could leave my things here?"

I hoped to learn my future fate from his answer. He thought a moment. Looked at me. Understood my wiles. Cleared his throat.

"All right. What's the point of carrying bundles back

and forth? We won't keep you long. You'll just sign a few papers and run home to Mama."

Now I knew what choking with happiness means. I was afraid to believe it.

The resourceful young man went to the landlady for the key. When the old woman came, she recognized me and clutched her heart. I must have been a terrible sight. She was crying so hard she couldn't put the key in the lock.

Ah, how good it was to be home! It smelled of Mama, warm, cozy. I didn't want to leave. My escort saw it and, feeling sorry for me, raised his voice in mock anger:

"You've gone limp with warmth. Move faster or you'll be late for lunch with Mama."

I just had time to glance at myself in the mirror. An unrecognizable face met me! I was a completely different person, with a new face. Two deep wrinkles ran from my nose to my lips. Extraordinary. That my face was green, dirty, the skin drawn, didn't matter. It was the look in the eyes that was striking, and it was this strange new look that made my face unrecognizable. A crust of dirt was congealing over my coat in the bitter cold. It didn't matter, I was very happy. I'd scrub myself clean, eat my fill, and get rid of the lice. Perhaps even my look would change back to what it was before.

Ah, how good it is to live! It hasn't been very long since they dragged me out of the punishment cell by the arms, and here I am, I've found my legs again, I'm capering with joy. I even smiled at my escort, but felt embarrassed at once to be smiling at a man with a mug like mine.

We trotted on. The snow crackled and sparkled in the sun, the bells jingled. It was so wonderful I couldn't believe it. Was it a dream?

*There*, however, I found frowning faces, rough voices. I had to fill out some papers and sign them. "Give me the papers, I'll sign anything you want, just let me go."

Again my legs trembled and my head swam. They handed me paper after paper through a partition, but the letters ran together, my hands shook, and I felt queasy. Swallowing hard, I asked:

"What's it all about? I can't make anything out, I don't feel well. May I sign without reading? I don't suppose it's my death sentence?"

"That would be a good thing," barked the malicious man behind the partition. "As it is, you have trouble with everyone—you get a horse for one, take another to the hospital, the third you can't lay a finger on . . ." And apparently driven to sudden fury by these recollections, he yelled:

"Come on, sign and get out of here, I don't have time to bother with you!"

My name was on the papers with some numbers—10, 15, and 25. Later I learned these were the terms possible for various offenses, such as ten years for going more than five kilometers beyond the town limits without permission, fifteen for going to another city or failing to report at the registry office, and twenty-five if caught "escaping."

At the time, I was profoundly indifferent. A hundred years or two hundred, so long as they let me go—before I got sick or fell in a faint again. I signed. But I was unable to stand up; my legs were cotton wool, everything swam in front of my eyes. The man behind the partition yelled:

"What are you sitting there for, my lady? Got nothing to do? There are people here with work to do. Or is something unclear? Come to register every two weeks, the date is on the identity card."

But when he saw I did not move, he said in an official voice:

"Citizeness, you are free."

With a great surge of willpower, the "free" citizen of the Union of Soviet Socialist Republics, obliged to register at the special office of the NKVD every two weeks, rose to her feet, and without taking a step, collapsed at the feet of her "liberator."

I came to on the street to the sound of bells. The same sleigh and the same fine young man were taking me home. He and the landlady had to carry me into Mother's house, and the landlady had to undress me. Whimpering with pity, she took off my boots, unfastened my coat, and laid me on the bed. She promised me hot tea right away, *bliny* and heaps of treats to come.

In my sleep, I heard a frightened cry. Then something heavy fell on me, smothering me. It was my beloved Mama. She had thought at first that thieves had broken into the house.

"Oh, how wonderful that it's you! I'd given up hope of seeing you. You see, I got a letter from Oleg, cautious, intelligent. I understood you'd been arrested. It'll soon be three months since I've heard anything from you or of you. But what a sight you are! By the way, who is this Oleg?"

How good it was to be home! Naturally, we sobbed with happiness. It could have been so much worse— nothing was known about Lev to that day, and Irochka had fallen ill en route and hadn't recovered yet; she was temporarily insane. And how did I feel? Fine, fine, couldn't be better. If only Mamochka would give me a little piece of plain bread and some hot tea, temporary insanity would be no threat.

"Oh my God, I don't have a thing for dinner yet, I just came back to see if maybe there was a letter from you or about you. I've been running here from work every day during breaks."

She found bread and butter and, oh! what delicious hot tea—really hot, for the first time in almost three months. Mama had to rush off to work, but found time to scold me.

"Why did you just sit there? Didn't I write you they'd arrested a lot of people? The clever ones came back on their own, but you had to stay in Leningrad, you couldn't live anywhere else. And you haven't told me who this Oleg is. Perhaps it's because of him you stayed there? But what a sight you are, a scarecrow with gray-green skin and eyes like a wolf!"

"But I am a wolf. And if you don't stop badgering me now, I'll bite. Oh, Mama, how good it is to be home. Run back to work, I'll get ready for the second half of the scolding. What institutes are there nearby?"

"Heavens above! Just look at you! What are you talking about? Who would let you in? When will you come to your senses?"

"Ha, ha, Mama, I've acquired resistance such as you've never dreamed of. When you come back this evening, I'll dance for you."

I didn't dance that evening, it's true, but watched while Mother got supper together and heated water. "You can't get in bed as you are, you ought to scrub for a month!" I grinned broadly with a satisfied, if green, face. And let myself be fed, washed, and have my hair trimmed a little. "What's this new-style hairdo? Is that the way they're doing their hair in Leningrad? Or did they tear your hair off?"

"I did it myself, Mama, self-service. I gnawed it with my teeth."

That was the completely satisfactory ending of my journey from Leningrad to—alas, not Moscow.

# Epilogue

I recovered quickly. Within a few days, I had taken over the housework, and a week later, I was able to go to market myself. Mama had a hard life, leaving early in the morning for work, which was a long walk away. Even for Siberia, the cold was intense that winter of 1953. She was paid a pittance, but she made ends meet with knitting orders, the sale of old clothes, and, from time to time, packages from my aunt. I longed to be useful.

Kansk had changed a great deal in the years I had been away. You no longer had to stand in long lines for bread. There wasn't enough white for everyone, it's true, but Mama had connections in the bread store, so they kept it for her under the counter. There was meat for sale in the market. Mama boasted that when the snow melted in spring, I'd be amazed to see real asphalt in some places. There was a regular bus now to the textile combine across the River Kan. There were more exiles, too.

I tried to cook something good for when Mama came home. I even learned to bargain in the marketplace, though I used to blush and stammer in my dialogue with the butcher, and spend a long time getting ready for it.

Mother and I immediately discovered our ideas clashed. The atmosphere in our hovel was sometimes red hot.

At last, I learned all about Papa. He had spent exactly ten years in prison, to the day. A year ago, in January, 1952, they had let him leave the camp, but brought him through Kansk without letting him see Mama. She only learned of it later. He was now living in a forest a few kilometers from Dzerzhinsk, working as a guard for the woodcutters, watching over wood in the forest. Mama had visited him, but it was very complicated. First you had to get permission from the NKVD, which, for her, was a real torture. Then you had to walk out on the highway to hitch a ride because there was no other transportation there. Contact with Papa was poor. Corresponding was very difficult because the loggers had to bring him his mail in the woods, and they often forgot to give him letters or forgot to put his letters to her in the box. Furthermore, they could meet only in Dzerzhinsk because she couldn't get to a mud hut in the middle of the woods, so he had to obtain permission to leave the forest. All in all, it was complicated.

"Has Papa changed much?"

"He's an old man, hair white as snow. But that doesn't matter, he's cheerful and seems healthy enough."

"How was it when you met? Did you cry?"

"At first, and then we had nothing to say. So many years had gone by. He kept asking about you and your sister."

"Did he tell you what it was like in camp?"

"No, and I didn't ask. What's there to tell? How people die like animals there?"

"But he survived, meaning he has something to tell."

"He was never resentful, never took anything to heart."

"Do you think that's why he survived?"

"I don't know. He said he was beaten more than once
and suffered terribly from hunger and cold. His feet were
frozen, and he did very heavy work, but he lasted out
ten years. He worried about you, suffered over you, was
always afraid you might be arrested. He remembers you
as very small, very thin. You were just eight then, you
know, and he was afraid you wouldn't survive."

"Can I go see him?"

"Probably. They grant permits to go there. But you'll
have to write him, which takes several weeks. Anyway,
don't think about that yet, you've hardly got body and
soul together."

"How long will Father have to live in the woods?"

"I don't know. We've both applied for permission
to live together here in Kansk. Either it's been refused
or they simply aren't answering."

"And when permission comes, will it say 'thanks to
the Fatherland's Party government'?"

"Don't be too clever. I already had to make signs
to you yesterday evening when you suddenly started
acting smart in front of strangers. Any one of them could
be an informer."

"Mama, they're your friends. And what are they?
Exiles themselves. Why the devil would they inform on
their own kind?"

"You're such a child. If they had a chance of getting
out of here, they'd sell their own mothers."

"One mustn't think of people like that."

"Come now, nobody asked these people if they
wanted to be informers."

"Well, you ought to know. How could anyone make
somebody into an informer if it goes against your nature,
if you wouldn't inform on your friends for anything in
the world?"

"Don't think you're more honest than the rest.
Another heroine! Before firing off your 'not for anything

in the world,' you might just stop to think a moment and maybe you'd understand how a person might not have the strength to refuse."

"But Mama dear, just suppose they call me in and order me to be their informer. Just picture it yourself. Friends come to see us in the evening, I deliberately direct the conversation to dangerous topics, and in the morning, run to inform the NKVD. Could that happen? Don't make me laugh, Mama. If they quartered me, I wouldn't stoop to that, I'd kill myself first."

Mother's lips quivered.

"Mama, what's the matter? Did I say something wrong again?"

"How could you say anything wrong? You always think you're so clever, that you understand absolutely everything about life. Let me tell you it will end badly for you and for all of us. In such questions you matter very little. Unfortunately, you just don't want to understand that, in spite of everything that's happened to you. What would you do, for instance, if they called you and told you to get ready to go to the far north? And you had two little children on your hands? Fine, at the time I had silk stockings and was able to buy my way out. But imagine a lone, helpless woman with little children being called out and told: 'You go north or you work for us.' She'd think it over a hundred times before refusing. Is it worth choosing to go die with your chilren in the tundra when there's a chance to survive?"

"Well?"

"What do you mean—well? Nobody would turn it down. There's no way to refuse. 'You don't want to cooperate with us?'—'What do you mean? I want to, but I don't know anybody, don't see anyone, I have small children, I wash floors.'—'We'll see that you meet people. We'll find the occasion and indicate the people we're interested in.'—'I'm sick, I have liver trouble, a bad stomach, I don't understand anything about politics, you'd do better to find someone else.'—'Does that mean you refuse to cooperate with us? You refuse to help uphold Socialist law? You aren't willing to exercise vigilance? We advise you to think it over. Come back tomorrow at the same time.' "

I listened, openmouthed.

"Mama, how do you know all this?"

"How do you think? Do you think I saw it in a movie? I lived through it in my own skin. In Dzerzhinsk. Remember that little boy who always taunted you, calling you a Lett and an exile? He was the son of the officer they dragged me to. And of course you don't remember how Musya, the woman we lived with then (by the way, she married very well), how Musya took care of me after my fainting fits. If it hadn't been for you two little mites, perhaps I would have killed myself then. But I found a way out."

"Aha, you see? Then it's possible to find a way out."

"Yes, and it's possible to get shot, too. Not everyone is that lucky and not everyone would have dared. You remember we got a package from your aunt in Palestine then? In Dzerzhinsk? Well, for just about everything in that package, that officer released me from becoming an informer, got my signature on a paper about 'not divulging state secrets,' and even helped us move to Kansk so we'd be out of sight. I was lucky to happen on a decent man. I could have gone to prison for bribery!"

"Decent! Why, he should have been shot for that. Mama, just think! An NKVD officer taking a bribe to free someone from informing. You've got to admit that makes a good story, doesn't it?"

"Fine, fine, just go tell someone that funny story. One should never tell you anything, your brains were always half-cocked. I'll be grateful to him until I die for helping me take a sin like that off my soul."

"That means someone else took your place. I wonder who?"

"Aha, now you've understood. So sit and hold your tongue."

"I've understood. In other words, if you hadn't gotten Aunty's package then, you'd be a stakhanovite stool pigeon now. Or if you'd refused, our white little bones, gnawed clean by wolves, would be scattered over the tundra."

"That's the way it is. But I beg you to keep quiet. And, please, never remind me of this. Get it through your head that for every forty exiles here there are four foremen. That's no riddle, it's absolutely official. Each foreman is, so to speak, responsible for the 'security' of his ten exiles, meaning he makes sure everyone's where he should be, he knows what everyone is thinking, and whether anyone is getting ready to escape. It's a sure thing that if he's asked what someone special like you is thinking, he won't make any effort to hide your frame of mind."

"I don't have a frame of mind. What frame of mind am I supposed to have! I've simply ceased to understand anything at all. And even if I did begin to have an inkling, there was nothing to be proud of in the fact that understanding came so late, and then only because I was personally involved. How is one to live with this? If you're so wise and rational, tell me what keeps this going? Stool pigeons, foremen? And whatever else there is? And if it weren't for these people 'upholding Socialist law,' as you put it, would everything fall apart?"

"I don't know. Don't ask, for God's sake, and don't think about it."

"But Mama, tell me, was it that way in Latvia, too?"

"What way?"

"Why, with exiles, informers, foremen?"

"How would I know! We weren't in exile there."

"And where did they send guilty people?"

"I don't know. Besides, you don't consider us guilty?"

"Aha, that means we are not guilty. See, see—and you hissing at me not to ask. You mean there weren't any exiles in Latvia?"

"Maybe there was nothing to be exiled for."

"And what were we exiled for?"

"We're socially dangerous elements."

"Dangerous to whom?"

"To society."

"What society?"

"The Socialist society."

"Who told you that?"

"Well, first, that's what they told us when we were arrested twelve years ago, and besides, take the trouble to read what's written on your special identity card, that's what it says."

"But in Latvian society—by the way, what kind of system was it?—in Latvian society, we weren't considered dangerous?"

"It was parliamentary, democratic. We weren't dangerous. On the contrary, we were quite respected."

"Oh, my God! We're not dangerous in a democracy, but in a Socialist society we're criminals. Now will you please tell me where the logic is in that?"

"Don't look for logic. And leave me in peace. I'm tired of your foolishness."

"All right, just one last question. Do you read the newspapers?"

"No. Who does?"

"Why?"

"Do you read them?"

"No."

"Why not? You're nineteen now, you're an intelligent girl."

"They never interested me. The only times I picked

up a paper was when I had to make a report on the international situation. Then I'd copy down the political news."

"Well, I haven't had to make reports."

"Are there any newspapers here?"

"Of course. I can bring you some from the technical school. Nobody there opens them. I can bring you new ones, no one will notice."

"Great. I'll make reports for you."

"Thanks a lot, that's all I needed. By the way, have you heard about the doctors' affair?"

"What doctors?"

"Is it possible you haven't heard? But, of course, that was after your arrest. It's awful! They arrested all the most important Jewish doctors, put them in prison, and accused them of sabotage, of supposedly poisoning a lot of people and plotting still another series of poisonings. It's a nightmare. Everyone says it's not for nothing, that they're preparing something against Jews in general."

"Where did you hear about this, in the marketplace?"

"Stupid, from the newspapers. And they broadcast it several times on the radio. Lately all they've talked about on the radio is vigilance. It was terrifying to pick up the newspaper. I still have those issues in the house. I brought them here from the technical school. I was afraid to read there for fear they'd say, 'She never reads, and now she's taking interest'—so I just put them in my bag and read them at home. My hair stood on end—nothing but Jewish names. And it sounded so frightening, as if they were giving warning, saying we'll all go the same way. It's hard to imagine what this is going to lead to, but when it's all that's talked about now in the newspapers and on the radio, believe me, something serious is brewing. They wouldn't talk about it to keep us informed. Read it yourself, I'll find the papers for you. Only for God's sake, if someone drops in tonight, don't start in on this subject, it's too dangerous now."

"All right, I'll keep quiet, but find these terrible newspapers. By the way, Mama, do you know why they keep broadcasting such mournful music? I wanted to get the time from the radio, and all they had was Tchaikovsky, and at the end of the *Sixth*, without a word, they started playing Beethoven's *Eroica*. Why?"

"Stalin is sick. They announced it on the radio this morning."

"Hooray, Mama! But why are you looking so horrified at me? I'm hardly going to put on a mournful mug in front of you. Oh, if they're playing that music in his honor, it must be serious. Maybe he croaked long ago and they still haven't decided what to do, so they're broadcasting music. Oh Mama, I have the feeling this is serious."

"Be sensible, my child, I beg you. The walls here have ears. People get shot for saying things like that, there's no doubt about it. You're playing with death. I'm not asking you to shed any heartfelt tears, but there's no reason to be so delighted either. Someone even worse could take his place."

"I'll be sensible and wise, I'll go around with the glummest expression possible, I won't say a single idiotic word to anyone, even Jack. But Mama, inside my guts, my own guts, don't I have the right to rejoice?"

"No. We don't know what lies ahead. And don't bury him before his time—this could be some sort of trick."

"Well, no-o-o, that's impossible. Tricks in something like that? They'd be afraid to so long as he is alive. And if he dies, who'll remember his sins? To the contrary, they'll build him a mausoleum more elegant than Lenin's with artificial ventilation and gilded toilets."

"How did you get so spiteful? How can you talk so disrespectfully about the dead? If he's dead . . ."

"And how many people are dead because of him? Honest, good, intelligent, educated—thousands, hundreds of thousands, maybe millions of lives ruined, and who remembers them with respect? Aren't there enough of them right here in Siberia?"

"You won't get another word out of me. But I can tell you, I don't like your new attitude at all. I don't know if it's the consequence of your 'free' life or if you only got bitter after you were arrested. Whichever it is, I assure you life will be very hard for you."

"Well, let it. The more difficult, the better."

"I don't get it."

"I'll understand more. I'll understand what keeps this going, how people live. What's it like for other people? Isn't it hard for them, too?"

"Yes, but for other reasons. They struggle to feed themselves, the family, to get something to wear, something to heat the stove with. They don't bother their heads with higher matters. It wouldn't hurt you to start thinking about how you intend to live either. I'm not saying you should run right out to look for work. No, no, rest, get well, you're still a sight, but your mind is getting unbalanced with idleness."

"All right, Mama, don't be angry, I've been home a whole week already. I'll think of something."

"I'm not angry. I'm afraid for you."

I wasn't used to reading newspapers, much less attentively.

VILE SPIES AND MURDERERS UNDER THE MASK OF PROFESSORS AND DOCTORS ran the bold-type headline in *Pravda* of the thirteenth of January, 1953. I read and reread the article about these vile spies and murderers several times, but still couldn't see just what they had done, what they were planning to do, or whose hirelings they were. It was, in any case, strange and frightening to read the word "Jewish" four times in a short article and the word "Zionist" twice, mixed with epithets like bourgeois nationalists, infamous monsters, terrorists, band of thugs, vermin, and traitors. The profusion of Jewish names was indeed sinister. It was hard to make sense out of the story. According to an announcement of the thirteenth of January, a group of doctor-poisoners had been arrested. The same communiqué reported that the murderers had already admitted killing comrades Zhdanov and Shcherbakov, and had confessed they were planning to put the military leaders out of action first in order to weaken our country's defenses. There was a list of the marshals and generals they were about to poison. Then why was actor Mikhoels included, when these mongrels were the paid agents of Anglo-American slaveowners and maneaters?

Mama was probably right. I don't understand anything about life. I'm spiteful, suspicious.

The same article spoke of the teachings of the immortal Lenin, and of Stalin, the father of the people. Both taught that the better off we and our Fatherland are, the sharper the struggle with the enemies of the people will be. What struggle? Was there so little vigilance among us? When even I was considered a criminal? Perhaps these doctors were no more guilty of "doing away with active leaders of the Soviet Union by medical sabotage" than the hundreds of completely innocent people I'd met in prison or "criminals" like my father? And why write about it? Why "expose" them? To make people fear and tremble?

Everyone was scared anyway. You had only to look at Mama. And was I any better? Wasn't it fear that kept me from telling Oleg about myself? I was afraid to tell even the person closest to me, the person I loved most. And tell him what? That I wasn't guilty of anything? That my parents weren't guilty of anything? Then why was I afraid to tell? Because I was afraid he'd denounce me? No, that's not true, I wasn't afraid of that, I simply didn't want to burden his conscience. I knew he was obliged to inform on me, but that he wouldn't, which would mean a blot on his conscience. Call that a conscience? Why the devil should he be obliged to report on me? To whom? And what? That I was alive, that I wasn't in Siberia, where, for some unknown reason, I was supposed to be? So then I was sparing his conscience. Loving him. And not trusting him. Can love exist without trust? But didn't he know there was something wrong about me anyway? He could have gotten it all out of me. If I'd confided in him, I would have loved him even more.

I felt so hurt, so bitter, that tears fell right on that terrible newspaper. How was I to live? Why was there suddenly this gulf between me and Oleg? What future did I have? Just then the radio played that music again, so gloomy, beautiful, and funereal, that I felt it was for me.

How much can anyone cry? Phoo, what a face! Swollen nose, red eyes, wet lips. "Music for me?" Bah, I want to live. Who would be the better for it if I killed myself? Was I the only one who had suddenly seen through all this horror and all these crying injustices? How did all the intelligent, mature people live? And how did the ones who created these injustices live? They're the ones who should kill themselves, not decent people. They're the killers. I'll live just in order to see these killers kill themselves with their own weapons.

I managed to convince myself and felt better. I took up the newspapers again. In another issue of *Pravda*, I found a review of a play called *Pavlik Morozov* at the Moscow Theater for Young Spectators. The play takes place in a village in the Ural taiga, where brave young Pioneer Pavlik Morozov denounces his own father, who

is removed from the village as a dangerous enemy—that
is, they exile or shoot him. And Pavlik is a hero. He
keeps on building up the kolkhoz even more zealously
and fearlessly disclosing the evil intentions of the enemy.

"And thunderous applause burst out in the hall as
the admiring eyes of the young spectators were fixed
on Pavlik. He appealed to their impressionable, youthful
minds." How could that be? The son denounces his father
and they shoot the father on the basis of the child's denun-
ciation—why, Pavlik is only twelve years old. Those
impressionable children were being taught to denounce
their own parents.

"Wake up! Stalin is dead! Sleeping like a log, covered
with newspapers, you'd do better to start getting yourself
a black armband."

"Congratulations, Mama, but if this turns out not to
be true, I'll denounce you and they'll shoot you."

"How can you be so silly?"

"I'm not being silly. That's what my Party and its
wise, now dead, leader and teacher teach me: Denounce!
Denounce! Denounce! Expose the foul monsters, mongrels, vermin. Come on, Mama, confess—what imperial-
ist intelligence service have you sold out to?"

"My God, what did I do to deserve such
punishment?"—and Mama burst into tears.

"What are you crying about? My frivolity or our
beloved Stalin?"

"Both. You don't understand a thing. Now *they* can
say anything they like, even that the Jews murdered
Stalin. Then they'll shoot us all, indiscriminately, big and
little, and exiles first."

"They can. *They* can do anything. But don't cry. Look
at me—see my swollen nose and red eyes?"

"Yes. How come?"

"I've been sobbing my heart out, sobbing about this

wretched life. I'm a fool, a complete fool. Instead of crying, one should bite and scratch. Tears will only get you an ugly face, there's no point in it. How did you find out Stalin kicked the bucket?"

"They announced it on the radio. But let's agree on this once and for all: If you don't want to drive me to the grave before my time, stop showing off. Just be as quiet as you can—you'll have a better chance of surviving. Promise me."

"I promise, Mama, in the glorious name of Pioneer Pavlik Morozov, that I'll conduct myself as quietly as possible and try to survive. But let's have supper, we don't have to starve out of solidarity. Let's make cocoa to honor the holiday. And I propose fried eggs, one whole egg per person. I feel the onset of unprecedented hunger and the surge of unprecedented spiritual strength. Hooray for the Fatherland and for Stalin!"

My poor mother, torn between laughter and sorrow, felt she ought to scold me, but she was amused. She didn't always manage to call me to order. She would roll her eyes, throw up her hands, and, all too often, call God to witness. "What do you torture me for?"

"Full stop. *Fini.* 'The cat's dead, her tail fell off, whoever says a word has to eat it. up . . .' " And having said the equivalent of "Cross my heart and hope to die," I enumerated all the unappetizing organs I would eat if I broke my promise not to comment and to try to survive.

Over fried eggs and cocoa, Mama told me how everyone had sobbed, unembarrassed, when Stalin's death was announced at the technical school. Even the men.

"And you?"

"What do you think? Naturally I sobbed, too."

"And Masha Mayatnik?"

"Yes."

"'The cat's dead, her tail fell off,'" I chanted. "Mama, could I go to the technical school with you to have a look at this Masha?"

"Of course. But there's nothing to see. She's a big, kind, country girl, washes floors beautifully. Much better than I do."

"She's an exile, too?"

"I already told you."

"Yes. I remember."

This Masha had once worked as a cleaning woman in a kolkhoz club in a village somewhere in Byelorussia. One day, while washing the floor, she carelessly bumped the pedestal holding a plaster bust of Stalin with her powerful behind, knocked it over, and broke it. Masha was sentenced by the *troika*. Taking her size into account, they gave her the minimum sentence: five years in prison, deprivation of rights, and exile for life. Masha did her five years without incident. She lost weight, understood nothing, and remained just as good. She was often pregnant. The last time she had to go to the hospital, it was with an infection from "self-abortion with a pendulum from a wall clock." Hence the nickname *Mayatnik*, meaning "pendulum." Mama had told me the story.

"They phoned us from the regional Party committee," Mama went on, "with the directive that tomorrow all workers and employees are to wear black armbands on the street and at work. Where'm I going to find a piece of black cloth?"

"I have some black cotton panties 'for certain times of the month' that I'm ready to sacrifice. And I'll be quiet—'The cat's dead.' I'll get you the panties now."

"Thank you."

That was the fifth of March, 1953.

The following day, Mama didn't come home for the noon meal and I suddenly became very worried. To be

honest, though I laughed it off in front of her, she had
passed on a good part of her fears to me with her predic-
tions.

Lord, has it started already? Are they taking Jews
right off the street?

I decided to wait until evening, then go look for her.
But she came back at her usual time.

"What happened, Mama?"

"They took me to the militia. I didn't notice your infer-
nal black panties had fallen off my sleeve, so they arrested
me—for not being in mourning. Yes, and please don't
look at me like such a wild beast, be good and remember
your stupid cat with the tail that fell off."


THE  BURNING


A few days later, my mother gave me a concert of
tears, prayers, and reproaches. It was Sunday. She had
been suspiciously silent since morning, which was not
like her at all. Then she began deliberately pacing in
front of me, though I wasn't at all in her way. She puffed
noisily, sat down to roll her cigarette of coarse tobacco
right in front of me, and struck matches nervously. I
saw it all, but was so deep in thought that I didn't take
it in at first. A threat was hanging in the air.

"Mama, what's wrong?"

Silence. Lips significantly compressed. That special
expression on her face.

"Bad news?"

Silence. That meant I was the problem. I tried to think
back, but I didn't seem to have any sins on my conscience.
The fuse had gone out. I'd been quiet. Not asking for
trouble. Not swaggering in front of people. Trying to
survive. Going nowhere. It's true I would soon have been
home for all of two weeks and was still of no use at

all. No one was going to hand me a job on a silver platter. But I didn't think that explained why Mama was puffing away.

Soon she erupted: "Isn't what's happened to you already enough? Look at yourself. You look like a wolf, you'll be sprouting fangs soon. Isn't it enough that we've been dragging around this accursed Siberia for twelve years and the end isn't in sight? Do you want to get us all shot?"

Mama said a lot of things. About my disobedience from the cradle on. And how I could have avoided a lot if I hadn't been so hardheaded and had listened to her advice. Why, she'd written to me to come at once. Why was it other children, who were as bad as I, even worse, didn't end up in prison, didn't traipse around in prison convoys, didn't go asking for trouble, and didn't make their poor mothers tremble with fear every day? Why, every day she approached the house in terror, afraid of not finding me there. And that's just what was going to happen if I didn't come to my senses. And this time I wouldn't get off so lightly if I were arrested.

"And there's no reason to smile so knowingly. You think you no longer have anything to fear, that you've been through it all, that now you can do as you please. I'm sure you got caught in Leningrad through your own foolishness. You probably boasted to someone that you once knew French, or had studied ballet and music, or something else of the sort."

"Don't be angry. I know what it's all about. Don't be afraid. Nothing worse is going to happen."

I understood now. Mama had found my notes, my "Journey from Leningrad to Siberia." I had been unable to deny myself the pleasure of putting down my impressions of the trip. Mama had given me that black notebook herself—and now she had apparently discovered it. And read it. And been terrified. Not because of what I'd seen and lived through, but because if she had found the notebook, someone else might, too. And then we'd be shot for certain.

She wouldn't sleep now. The house would be searched from top to bottom. There was no one to leave the notebook with.

Mother sobbed and stirred up the fire in the stove. The notebook had gotten damp in the corner behind the radio where I'd hidden it. It didn't want to burn. Bustling about and merrily blinking teary eyes, Mama offered to bake *draniki,* my beloved grated potato pancakes. She was pleased with my obedience.

I always loved watching a fire; it was not for nothing Oleg called me a fire-worshiper. And there smoldered the story I so much wanted to tell people one day. I was very anxious to remember it. As I watched the fire, I convinced myself that things like that are not forgotten, that nothing would obscure the journey I had begun as a sparrow and ended as a fanged wolf. And the faint hope glimmered that this could not last forever. That there would be an end to this perversion. And that there must be places on earth where people are not shot for the truth.